TRAVERSING WALLS

 **68** Activities
On and Off the Wall

Jim Stiehl ▣ Dan Chase
University of Northern Colorado

Human Kinetics

Library of Congress Cataloging-in-Publication Data

Stiehl, Jim.
Traversing walls : 68 activities on and off the wall / Jim Stiehl, Dan Chase.
    p. cm.
Includes bibliographical references.
ISBN-13: 978-0-7360-6777-5 (soft cover)
ISBN-10: 0-7360-6777-9 (soft cover)
1. Rock climbing. I. Chase, Dan, 1972- II. Title.
GV200.2.S753 2007
796.522'3--dc22

                        2007023795

ISBN-10: 0-7360-6777-9
ISBN-13: 978-0-7360-6777-5

Acquisitions Editor: Gayle Kassing, PhD; **Developmental Editor:** Ray Vallese; **Assistant Editor:** Derek Campbell; **Copyeditor:** Jan Feeney; **Proofreader:** Bethany J. Bentley; **Permission Manager:** Dalene Reeder; **Graphic Designer:** Bob Reuther; **Graphic Artist:** Carol Smallwood; **Cover Designer:** Keith Blomberg; **Photographer (cover):** Neil Bernstein; **Photographer (interior):** Neil Bernstein, except where otherwise noted; photos on pages 5 (figure 1.2) and 122 courtesy of Jim Stiehl; photos on pages 48-50 courtesy of Sportime Physical Education/School Specialty, Inc.; **Visual Production Assistant:** Joyce Brumfield; **Photo Office Assistant:** Jason Allen; **Art Manager:** Kelly Hendren; **Illustrators:** Tim Offenstein, Argosy (figures on p. 133); **Printer:** Versa Press

We thank Mike McMahon and Northview Elementary School in Rantoul, Illinois, for assistance in providing the location for the photo shoot for this book. We also thank the following students for appearing in the photos: Charles Cargo, Eli Dawdy, Harley Denny, Nathan Hutton, Ryan Koch, Niesha Mendoza, Cree Noble, Briana Sampson, Jose Villegas, and Ashley Walp.

Printed in the United States of America   10 9 8 7 6 5 4 3 2 1

Human Kinetics   Web site: www.HumanKinetics.com

United States: Human Kinetics
P.O. Box 5076
Champaign, IL 61825-5076
800-747-4457
e-mail: humank@hkusa.com

Canada: Human Kinetics
475 Devonshire Road Unit 100
Windsor, ON N8Y 2L5
800-465-7301 (in Canada only)
e-mail: orders@hkcanada.com

Europe: Human Kinetics
107 Bradford Road
Stanningley
Leeds LS28 6AT, United Kingdom
+44 (0) 113 255 5665
e-mail: hk@hkeurope.com

Australia: Human Kinetics
57A Price Avenue
Lower Mitcham, South Australia 5062
08 8372 0999
e-mail: info@hkaustralia.com

New Zealand: Human Kinetics
Division of Sports Distributors NZ Ltd.
P.O. Box 300 226 Albany
North Shore City
Auckland
0064 9 448 1207
e-mail: info@humankinetics.co.nz

To our loved ones, Julie and Lisa.
We may be home late—again.

CONTENTS

ACTIVITY FINDER

96.5233
58557

PREFACE

Traverse-wall climbing is quickly growing in popularity, and it's easy to understand why. Although not employing the specialized techniques and equipment (such as ropes and harnesses) necessary for tall wall climbing and rock climbing, traverse-wall climbing is exhilarating, challenging, healthy, and fun. Traverse-wall climbing, sometimes referred to as traversing (climbing across) and bouldering, emphasizes movement close to the ground and generally involves more horizontal than vertical movement. If a climber falls while traversing, the fall is limited to relatively short distances. In addition, a partner, or spotter, is trained to protect the falling climber from landing badly on the landing surface. As noted by first-grader Brennan (First Ascent climbing brochure, 2006), "It's cool that you go sideways!"

Another reason for the rising popularity of traverse-wall climbing is that it tends to be a learned skill, requiring less natural ability than many other sports, and it relies more on technique and balance than brute strength. Finally, the appeal of traverse-wall climbing can be attributed, in part, to the outstanding design and construction of today's affordable, attractive, and durable traversing walls and landing surfaces.

Increasingly, schools are incorporating traversing walls into their physical education programs. Kids 7 to 14 years old made up the largest percentage of new climbers over the past several years. Many of these schools are benefiting from the federal government's Physical Education for Progress (PEP) program, which provides funds to purchase fitness and sports equipment and to train teachers in innovative physical education programs. Since the program was initiated in 2001 (approved by U.S. Congress in December 2000), the PEP program has provided treadmills, heart rate monitors, inline skates, and other equipment including traversing walls to help initiate, expand, and improve physical education programs for school-age youngsters. As youngsters stretch and grab their way across appropriately demanding traverse routes, they enhance their physical proficiency (balance, strength, and coordination) while confronting cognitive challenges and building interpersonal skills. Traversing walls easily include all standards recommended by the National Association for Sport and Physical Education (2004), such as skillful movement, regular participation in physical activity, physical fitness, and responsible personal and social behavior.

Although many of the activities in *Traversing Walls: 68 Activities On and Off the Wall* were designed for elementary- and middle-school youngsters, these activities can be adjusted for other climbers with various intentions. College students, for example, use traverse walls for their physical and mental challenge and to relieve stress. Rock climbers use them to hone technique and stay in condition during inclement weather. Beginners use them to learn basic techniques without straying too far from the ground. Moreover, some people consider traversing to be a sport in its own right and view traverse-wall climbing as a leisure and social activity. Regardless of the participant's age or intention, traversing activities can boost participation and motivation.

Creative Activities

We're confident that, like most facilitators of traverse walls, you want to offer climbing experiences and challenges that are appropriate for the interests and abilities of your clientele. However, specific games and activities for traverse walls are difficult to find. A limited number of traversing activities are available from wall manufacturers, in articles, and at workshops. In another book, *Climbing Walls: A Complete Guide* (Stiehl & Ramsey, 2005), we present information about wall design and construction, operational and emergency procedures, climbing routes, maintenance and care of climbing walls and equipment, and sample forms and checklists. We also provide a few wall-tested activities to challenge and motivate climbers. But teachers asked for more examples and ideas about traversing activities. Therefore, this book is primarily about using innovative and engaging activities that can maximize the benefit and increase the enjoyment and challenge of using traverse walls.

The contents of *Traversing Walls: 68 Activities On and Off the Wall* are meant to be suggestive rather than exhaustive. You can expand on the ideas almost without end. For example, a popular traversing activity is Add-On (see page 62 in chapter 3). In this activity, after successfully copying someone else's movements, the climber adds another movement to be copied. To introduce variety and challenge to this game, you can do any of the following:

- Require certain moves (for example, the climber must reach past the next nearby hold).
- Prohibit certain moves (for example, the climber can't touch orange holds).

- Apply specific rules (for example, the climber must reverse direction at a designated point).
- Turn it into a game (for example, you can play a version of the familiar elimination game Horse, in which climbers acquire letters when they fail to copy previous movements).

With some direction and ingenuity, you can also turn a basic activity such as Add-On into a more complex game. Here are examples:

- Mark holds with letters, and have climbers spell their names or complete a crossword puzzle.
- Mark holds with numbers, and have climbers add them to reach a particular total or solve a math problem.
- Mark holds with the names of locations, and have climbers visit the birthplaces of U.S. presidents or world leaders in order.

In fact, you can merge virtually any intellectual ability, academic task, popular game, or equipment with climbing and traversing activities. Teachers who reviewed this book and our previous work have devised many ingenious variations for climbers. For example, some have developed games that feature numbers, letters, or shapes affixed to the traverse wall. Others have created maps that direct climbers along specified routes. Using this technique, you can make a traverse wall into a map of the United States, a golf course, or a diagram of the night sky. Still other teachers have collaborated with their colleagues and incorporated math or geography into their climbing activities.

Organization

We have organized *Traversing Walls: 68 Activities On and Off the Wall* into seven chapters and an appendix.

In chapter 1, we introduce the benefits of traversing activities and discuss ways in which the activities can align with content standards and program goals. This chapter includes useful terminology about climbing techniques and holds, some warm-ups, and general safety considerations. It also presents strategies for creating endless variations of traversing activities, along with inexpensive ways to modify your existing wall to make climbing more challenging and interesting.

In chapter 2, we offer lead-up activities and exercises that are performed on the floor rather than on a wall. They're easy to apply in any situation and can be set up on almost any indoor or outdoor surface. Some of the activities and exercises use equipment to enhance strength, balance, or both. Others involve a series of balance blocks or dome cones arranged in patterns that simulate the moves made while climbing. By learning not only to maintain good balance and body position but also to communicate, solve problems, and support each other, students prepare for success on the wall. You can offer the activities and exercises in stations and have students rotate among them to face various challenges.

In addition, once the first students begin traversing, the floor stations continue to engage other students who are waiting for their turns on the wall. This benefit is particularly important because teachers frequently tell us, "I have 30 kids in my class, and only a few of them can use the wall at a time. What do I do with the *rest* of my students?"

The remaining chapters offer scores of activities and variations, organized by theme:

- Chapter 3 presents wall versions of well-known games, such as Simon Says, Go Fish, and Limbo.
- Chapter 4 features activities based on math and numbers.
- The activities in chapter 5 involve word and letter puzzles.
- Chapter 6 takes students around the world, offering activities that simulate travel to various destinations.
- Chapter 7 presents activities based on healthy living, such as finding foods to complete MyPyramid, assembling the bones of a human skeleton, and choosing pathways that correspond to healthy choices.

Many of the activities use equipment and materials such as hoops, dice, and playing cards. All of the activities promote a healthy, fun, productive learning environment in which everyone can participate and succeed. And a large number of activities promote cooperative problem solving between climbers on the wall and students on the floor.

Knowing that no single activity or approach is right for everyone, we wrote *Traversing Walls: 68 Activities On and Off the Wall* with the intention of offering a variety of creative opportunities for climbers of various ages and abilities. We don't have all the answers, but we hope the ideas and suggestions in this book will help you develop further activities that are geared toward your specific resources and students. We encourage you to be creative and flexible and to think of other ways to use traversing to engage your students, challenge their personal abilities, and provide them with satisfying, enjoyable climbing experiences.

ACKNOWLEDGMENTS

Writing a book requires help and support from others. We thank the scores of youngsters who cheerfully tried out and improved many of the activities and who are part of the next generation of traversing enthusiasts. In addition, the editorial staff at Human Kinetics have been most helpful in their dealings with us during preparation of the manuscript for publication. For many years, Scott Wikgren has furnished stalwart backing for anything innovative that will serve youngsters through physical activity. Gayle Kassing has provided relentless encouragement and faith in our work. Derek Campbell worked diligently to ensure that this book developed into a logical and valuable extension of our previous book on climbing walls. Ray Vallese has offered much-needed advice, careful scrutiny, and sound criticism throughout the entire project. Indeed, Ray's wit and attention to detail permeates this book. Thanks also to the photographers and illustrators whose work brings clarity and excitement to many of the activities.

Our special thanks to Fran Zavacky for her off-wall lead-up activities and to Jeff Steffen and Jeff McNamee for introducing us to the many benefits of dome cones. Their combined contributions provide prospective climbers with firm footing before actual climbing. As both a longtime colleague and climbing partner, Jeff Steffen has been particularly helpful and reassuring with his insight and creative input.

Finally, we are most grateful to our families, especially our wives, Julie and Lisa, who aided in constructing and playing on our traverse wall. We appreciate their kindness, wisdom, and enduring patience.

Getting Started

Traverse walls (also called climbing walls) are inherently appealing, so it's not surprising that instructors and prospective climbers are eager to get right to it. However, successful climbing requires a preliminary understanding of some fundamentals, plus an opportunity to explore and practice them. Someone who is new to climbing traverse walls and who doesn't fully understand the variables can be in an unsafe position. Conversely, knowledge of the fundamentals substantially reduces the risk of injury. The chief aim of *Traversing Walls: 68 Activities On and Off the Wall* is to provide you with sound basics, not to elaborate on more advanced or complex specifics of climbing. Climbing is a game of control, of mental and physical achievement. It also can be "a metaphor for life itself. There is the aspiration and the uncertainty, the journey and the risk, the success and its concomitant satisfaction. . . . We win here and we know that we can win elsewhere" (Mellor, 1997, p. 17). As instructors, we are obligated to maximize the satisfaction and adventure of climbing and to minimize any potential risk.

What This Book Is and Is Not

No single book can adequately address all of the intricacies of climbing. For example, topics such as designing and constructing climbing walls, selecting and placing holds, teaching specific climbing techniques, and managing a climbing program are beyond the scope of this book. In the appendix you can find sources for more information on those and other relevant climbing topics. Also, this book does not focus on teaching and coaching per se, and we don't claim to offer a movement-based curriculum. Rather, we present "kid-tested" activities that you can use in ways that promote your goals.

Furthermore, over the years we have read many books on physical activity. Most of them have been helpful but lack one or two qualities that an activity leader desires in such a book: brevity and creative modifications.

Brevity

Presumably, anyone who consults a book of activities wants to gain as much information as possible in the least amount of time. Many books of activities are voluminous, gorged with unnecessary details. *Traversing Walls: 68 Activities On and Off the Wall* is for those who desire many ideas and activities that can be read and understood quickly. We supplement the main activities with brief explanations of variations.

Creative Modifications

It's difficult or impossible to invent absolutely new activities all of the time. Frequently, activities that are called "new" are simply modifications of older ideas, some of which become more interesting than the original. Such modifications are not hard to make. It's merely necessary to consider some of the elements common to many activities, and then adjust these using a few simple strategies presented later in this chapter. There are limitless possibilities, and enough of them are sufficiently useful to create all the activities you'll ever need.

Benefits of Traverse Wall Activities

As noted elsewhere (for example, Stiehl & Ramsey, 2005), climbing provides various benefits:

- An outlet through which children can focus their natural disposition to climb
- Experiences of genuine success for able and less-able people
- An exciting option for improving fitness
- Physical challenges, mental challenges, and stress relievers
- A means of promoting teamwork and leadership
- A fun leisure activity

It's also easy to understand how climbing activities can address each of the National Association for Sport and Physical Education's physical activity content standards as a basis for curriculum development. The standards are summarized as follows (NASPE, 2004):

- Standard 1: Demonstrates competency in motor skills and movement patterns.
- Standard 2: Demonstrates understanding of movement concepts, principles, and strategies.
- Standard 3: Participates regularly in physical activity.
- Standard 4: Achieves and maintains a health-enhancing level of physical fitness.
- Standard 5: Exhibits responsible personal and social behavior.
- Standard 6: Values physical activity for health, enjoyment, challenge, self-expression, and social interaction.

Moving Into the Future: National Standards for Physical Education, 2nd Edition (2004) reprinted with permission from the National Association for Sport and Physical Education (NASPE), 1900 Association Drive, Reston, VA 20191, USA.

These standards are used to define what a student should know and be able to do as a result of participating in an effective physical education program. However, they readily apply to recreational programs in which people use traverse walls solely to enjoy the satisfaction of climbing. Very simply put, whether the goals are educational or recreational, climbing traverse walls is alluring in many ways.

Applying the physical activity standards, climbing activities call for acquiring and applying new and enjoyable skills, often leading to increased participation in physical activity. Body control, precision of movement, eye–hand and eye–foot coordination, spatial awareness, and balanced weight transfers are skills and patterns promoted through climbing. In addition, cognitive skills such as planning, decision making, and problem solving are routine aspects of climbing. Resting, using counter-pressure techniques, deciphering a route, and planning moves in advance all present ongoing individual mental challenges as well as opportunities to engage in cognitive strategies with peers.

The vigorous nature of many climbing activities requires a health-enhancing level of physical fitness. Strengthened back, leg, shoulder, and forearm muscles, along with increased endurance and flexibility, are important fitness outcomes. Furthermore, supporting others in their attempts to climb demands a responsible and tolerant attitude. That is, participants must be concerned about their own welfare as well as the welfare of others, taking into account one another's interests, strengths, and limitations.

Finally, climbing activities afford opportunities for using a range of abilities in a supportive, inclusive environment. With each new climbing activity, the level of difficulty can be adjusted to suit the needs and abilities of each person, thereby allowing the climber to gain personal performance feedback. In addition, team activities include challenges where the level of communication and problem solving becomes a measure of success.

Climbing lends itself to the broad outcomes expected in a high-quality physical education program. And although climbing activities are an important means of curriculum extension and enrichment, they shouldn't be viewed as a replacement for more traditional physical education activities.

Useful Climbing Terminology

Some traversing enthusiasts use technical terms that can be strange and confusing to newcomers. For example, we once heard an instructor exclaim, "Let's avoid all beta smack today." The phrase could puzzle or even intimidate people who are unfamiliar with its meaning. ("Smack" refers to using an unsupportive, even taunting, means of presenting "beta," which is slang for information about a route's holds or sequence of climbing moves, derived from the old Betamax video recorders.)

The following terms are commonly associated with traverse walls and appear throughout the book. The list is by no means exhaustive, and additional terminology might apply to more advanced techniques and more elaborate traverse walls.

Parts of the Wall

The following terms deal with elements found on the traverse wall.

A **bucket** is an in-cut hold that is easily grasped.

A **crimper** (also called a *pinch* or *edge*) is a small knob with a dime-edge surface. The hold presents either a very thin edge or may be rounded with a slight indentation.

A **horn** is a rounded, knoblike hold.

A **jug** (also called a **bucket**) is a hold that is large and easy to grasp.

A **pocket** is a hold into which you can place your fingers and sometimes your entire hand.

A **sloper** is a large, severely rounded hold that resembles the bottom of a bowl.

Footwork

The following terms deal with movement of the feet.

Edging is using the inside or outside edge of your shoe to stand on a small-edged foothold (figure 1.1).

Doing a **heel hook** means placing the inside part of your heel on a protruding hold (figure 1.2).

Smearing involves placing as much of your shoe sole as possible against a surface (the wall itself) to obtain enough friction for support (figure 1.3).

FIGURE 1.1 Edging.

FIGURE 1.2 Heel hook.

FIGURE 1.3 Smearing.

Handholds

The following terms deal with placement of the hands.

An **open grip** involves your whole hand (including the palm, fingers, and thumb) to grasp a big or rounded feature (figure 1.4).

A **cling grip** is using your hand more like a claw to grab a pocket (figure 1.5).

A **pinch grip** occurs when you use your thumb and fingers like a lobster claw to squeeze two surfaces toward each other (figure 1.6).

A **sidepull** involves pulling sideways on a handhold that is vertically or diagonally oriented (figure 1.7).

A **mantle** involves stepping up with one foot and pressing down with your palm for a vertical boost (figure 1.8).

An **undercling** is grabbing a hold with your palm up (figure 1.9).

FIGURE 1.4 Open grip.

FIGURE 1.5 Cling grip.

FIGURE 1.6 Pinch grip.

FIGURE 1.7 Sidepull.

FIGURE 1.8 Mantle.

FIGURE 1.9 Undercling.

Fundamental Climbing Techniques

Climbing is natural and easy, but the key to good climbing—that is, climbing where neither strength nor energy is wasted—is efficiency. Good climbing technique comes from understanding some basic concepts and consistently performing them on the wall.

Climb With Your Eyes First

This old saying means to scan the wall to find the best possible route or hold. In other words, plan each move before executing it. This may require visualizing a move and rehearsing it mentally before actually moving.

Start With Your Legs

Initiate moves by pushing with your legs rather than pulling with your arms. Use your legs and feet more than your arms and hands, because your legs are stronger and won't tire as quickly. Climbing can quickly sap the fittest muscles, so it's crucial to conserve energy and reduce unnecessary moves.

Keep Your Weight Over Your Feet

Keep your body vertical. When your body is vertical, you can use gravity to force your weight down on your shoes, permitting maximum friction.

Employ Good Footwork

Take small steps—two small steps are less tiring than one big step—and place each foot deliberately on the best part of a hold. Then, by initiating weight shifts with the lower body, fluidly shift your weight over your foot before moving to the next point of contact. Some climbers call this "quiet feet." With practice, you'll find support on even the tiniest holds.

Maintain Three Points of Contact

To maximize your steadiness, use a combination of hands and feet to maintain three points of contact with the wall. Thus, if moving your left hand, don't move your right hand or either foot. This might not be possible on more difficult routes. However, maintaining fewer than three points of contact will compromise your balance, forcing you to make difficult adjustments to regain stability.

Rest on the Wall

Pick a hold that is as big as possible and hang from it with a straight arm or stand on it with a straight leg. Straight arms and legs place more weight on bones, which don't tire, than on muscles. To reduce tension and get your blood flowing, let one limb at a time dangle free and shake it. Relax and take a few regulated, deep breaths.

General Safety Concerns

To ensure that climbing remains exciting, challenging, and rewarding, reinforce the various aspects of safety. For example, warming up the muscles before climbing can prevent injuries resulting from overstretching while on the wall, and students can learn to be responsible for each other by acting as spotters.

Some of the floor and wall activities in chapters 2 through 7 identify safety considerations that are specific to the action or the equipment. In this chapter, we cover general safety concerns that apply to all climbing activities. Following these guidelines can help reduce the risk of injury.

Warm-Ups

Before climbing, get the blood flowing and get muscles and joints loose and supple. Stretching is the best way to prevent muscle and tendon injuries while also increasing flexibility. However, warming up first with some brief cardio activity is more advisable than stretching while the muscles are cold. Stretching while cold can cause pulled muscles and tendon injuries. Thus, prior to stretching, students should first warm up by jumping rope, doing jumping jacks, running in place, or performing some other simple cardio activity. In larger groups, partnered stretching allows climbers to warm up together, but they must communicate with each other about any pain so they don't risk injury by overstretching.

Descriptions of several useful stretches appear on pages 10 and 11.

Stretches

Repeat each stretch on both sides of the body.

Inner Thighs, Hips, and Buttocks (figure 1.10). While sitting on the floor, extend your left leg and cross your right foot over your left knee. Lean forward into the legs to stretch your right hip and the buttocks of the bent leg. To stretch the inner thighs, shift position so that the legs are spread apart in a "V" and lean forward.

Hamstrings (figure 1.11). While sitting, extend both legs and flex your feet so your toes point toward the ceiling. Stretch forward and, if possible, grasp your toes and pull them toward your body.

FIGURE 1.10 Inner thighs, hips, and buttocks stretch.

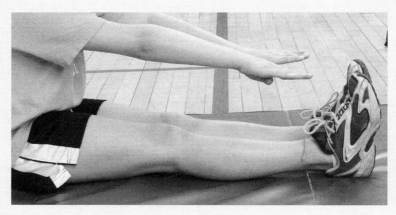

FIGURE 1.11 Hamstring stretch.

Shoulder (figure 1.12). To stretch your right shoulder while sitting or standing, pull your right arm across your body and press it against your chest with your left arm.

Forearm (figure 1.13). Extend your right arm in front of your body with the palm down and the elbow slightly bent. With your left hand, pull your right hand down so that it bends at the wrist and the palm ends up facing your body. To stretch just a bit more, curl the fingers of your right hand inward, toward your palm.

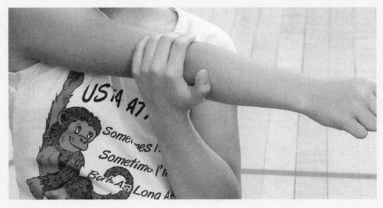

FIGURE 1.12   Shoulder stretch.

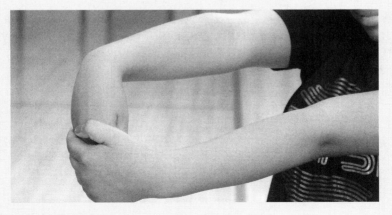

FIGURE 1.13   Forearm stretch.

A SAFE Environment

When conducting traversing activities, you must supervise the climbers, evaluate their abilities, maintain the fall surface, and maintain the equipment. The acronym SAFE can help you remember these four considerations.

S: Supervision

Are you supervising the participants appropriately? For example, do you move around the area and check to make sure that climbs proceed safely? Are you knowledgeable about climbing, basic safety rules, local protocols, and finding answers to important questions? Do you rely on professionals for advice and guidance? Do signs, wall coverings, or other elements prevent improper access when you or another supervisor is not present?

A: Ability

Is the design of the traverse wall, including its holds and routes, appropriate to the climbers' ability? Are your supervisor's expectations appropriate for the group?

F: Fall Surface

Is the surface area in front of the wall clean and free of debris? Is the surface area free of obstacles such as ladders and chairs? Is the material of the surface area adequate for cushioning falls? (Gymnastics mats and carpeting work well. If those materials aren't available, examine the surface area carefully and determine if it could be improved.)

E: Equipment

Is the equipment proper and maintained? For instance, is the equipment periodically repaired, replaced, or upgraded? Are good records kept of equipment changes and inspections? Are new routes installed periodically, and are old routes removed? Is a maximum height limit identified (such as with tape, a painted line, or established protocol), especially for younger climbers?

Adapted from the S.A.F.E. Model (TM) National Program for Playground Safety.

Rules for Climbers

While the instructor must ensure a SAFE environment, the participants share in the responsibility for overall climbing safety. Anyone using the traverse wall should understand and adhere to established rules and protocols:

- Make sure there's a safe landing area—no cushion, no climbing.
- Don't climb without supervision.

- Always use a spotter. (See the next section for details.)
- Don't climb higher than established limits; for example, your feet should be no higher than 3 feet (about 1 meter) off the ground.
- Don't leap to the floor; jump lightly away from the wall, even during a fall.
- Don't wear bracelets, long earrings, necklaces, or other objects that might cause injury.
- Don't rush or crowd a climber in front of you.
- After completing a climb, help spot another climber.

Spotters

Throughout this book, we emphasize the importance of creating a reassuring and encouraging atmosphere. Students not only need to observe climbing rules for their own safety, but they also must provide an environment that is physically and emotionally safe for others.

A spotter is someone who is trained to stand behind a climber and who physically helps to protect a falling climber from landing badly on the landing surface. Falls can be harmful to both faller and spotter alike. Teaching spotting is especially important; often, students don't realize the importance of spotting until they have to support a falling climber. Therefore, instruct spotters to focus continuously on the climber. Although poor spotting is unsafe and can have detrimental effects on a climber, good spotting results in increased confidence and a greater sense of trust among group members. Actively promote good spotting, which includes prohibiting any teasing or joking about not protecting someone. Encourage pride in becoming a good spotter.

The purpose of good spotting is to absorb part of a climber's fall, not to catch the climber by taking the whole of a climber's weight during a fall. Good spotting position requires a balanced stance (figure 1.14). A spotter's feet should be about shoulder-width apart, with one foot positioned slightly in front of the other. Knees should be flexed a bit to absorb impact, while arms and hands are extended with the palms facing toward the climber and at the level of the climber's waist. Teach spotters to move along the floor as the climber moves along the wall and be ready for a fall at any time. Spotters shouldn't make physical contact with the climber unless a fall occurs. If that happens, a spotter should cushion rather than catch the fall.

Spotters and climbers must communicate with clear, specific statements or commands to make sure both people are ready before climbing begins. The exchange can be as simple as the following:

FIGURE 1.14 Students should practice good spotting techniques.

Climber: "Ready?"
Spotter: "Ready."
Climber: "Climbing."
Spotter: "Climb."

Designate at least one spotter for each climber. In addition, ensure that spotters are competent and comfortable with their responsibilities and that they are placed appropriately—in other words, a spotter and a climber should be roughly the same size.

Modifying Activities

This book contains many ready-to-use activities, but you can and should create your own as well. A few simple strategies can help you invent appropriate and safe activities and variations. This is especially important when working with people who have a physical impairment. For example, the size and placement of holds can invite or deter participation. Similarly, moves, routes, and rules can be welcoming or dispiriting.

Change the Components

By considering the various components common to all climbing activities, any activity can be changed to create variations that might be more interesting, more challenging, or more inviting. The components combine to form a blueprint for examining any climbing activity, and we can organize them into categories:

- **Participants.** Vary whether participants climb individually, in pairs, or in teams.
- **Organizational pattern.** Are students randomly scattered? Are they arranged in a circle formation? At designated stations?
- **Equipment.** Vary the size, shape, and location of the wall holds, plus the use of other equipment such as beanbags, marking tape, hoops, worksheets, dice, and spinners.
- **Movements.** Vary whether climbers move deliberately, quickly, or in a manner to stress balance, strength, or flexibility.
- **Rules.** Vary the climbing rules. For example, a climber can touch only certain holds or must imitate the movements of a previous climber.

Following are some ideas for different variations you could make for these five components:

Participants

- Pairs (climber and spotter); teams
- Gender (coed and separate)
- Size (matched and different)
- Birthday (January and June; 1st to 10th of month)
- Ability (matched, different)
- Heavier and lighter
- Name begins with A to F, name begins with G to L, and so on
- Wearing something blue, yellow, and so on
- Prefer dogs or cats, plain or peanut M&Ms

Organizational Pattern (How to Arrange)

- Randomly scattered
- Two groups facing one another
- At stations
- In a line, behind one another

Equipment (Objects, Materials)

- Holds (size or type, placement, color)
- Hurdles, mats, ropes, hoops
- Balls, beanbags
- Spinner, dice, playing cards (figure 1.15a)
- Milk cartons, bleach bottles
- Balloons
- Music
- Worksheets, score sheets
- Colored tape, masking tape
- Index cards (figure 1.15b)

a

b

FIGURE 1.15 Affix *(a)* playing cards or *(b)* index cards near handholds.

Movements

- Types
    - Support weight, apply force
    - Turn, twist, balance, stretch
    - Catch, throw
- Directions
    - Forward, backward
    - Curved, zigzag, straight
    - Right and left, up and down
- Relationships
    - Mirroring
    - Contrasting
- Near and far
    - From others
    - From equipment or objects
    - Above, below, alongside others or objects
- Other
    - To music
    - To stories, poems, words
    - To beat pattern

Rules and Limits

- Acceptable and unacceptable movements
- Time limit (3 minutes)
- Turn limit (after adding a movement)
- Scoring: 2 points if they touch all holds
- Cannot touch 2 same-colored holds in succession
- Only 2 people moving at once
- Cannot move backward
- Move without dropping object

As an example, let's look at ways to change Add-On (chapter 3), a simple activity in which climbers try to copy the route of the previous climber and then add a new move to the sequence. They keep taking turns until they can't complete the route. The winner is the final climber who is able to copy the sequence and add to it. Variations of Add-On can include changes in several categories.

Here are some sample variations in the rules:

- Climbers must follow an exact sequence. For example, each begins with the right foot on a red hold, the left foot on a green hold, the right hand using a small pinch grip, and the left hand underclinging a blue hold. This change significantly increases the challenge of the activity, because climbers not only follow a prescribed route but also use specific holds on that route.
- Climbers can use any foothold, but they must follow a prescribed sequence of handholds. This change decreases the challenge presented in the first variation.

Here are sample variations to the rules and the organization of participants:

- Spotters can assist climbers by reminding them of what kinds of holds are allowed and giving suggestions about where to move next.
- Spotters can't coach climbers at all.
- Split the group into small teams of three or four climbers. Each team takes its turn to play Add-On for 10 minutes, and members record their progress on a worksheet. After all teams have had a chance to play, teams swap routes and try to beat other teams' previous scores.

The following are sample variations that involve changes to rules, participants, and movement:

- Climbers must add to the sequence as requested by the students on the floor. For example, a student on the floor can ask the current climber to extend the route by moving to the left rather than up, down, or to the right.
- A more difficult but fun variation is Three Touch. For example, upon hearing someone say "Right foot three," the climber must touch three holds with the right foot before his or her next move. Also, any holds touched with the right foot cannot be used in the next move.

Here are sample variations that also involve equipment:

- Mark a route with colored tape, thus minimizing reliance on memory.
- Award bonus points to a climber who adds a movement that results in the discovery of a hidden treasure, such as a playing card affixed to the wall near a particular hold, which is revealed to be a "valuable" face card.

- Tape a hoop flat against the wall and declare that climbers must use (or avoid) holds that fall within the hoop, perhaps in sequence.
- Use a specially designed hold to affix a hoop to the wall vertically, horizontally, or diagonally, and declare that climbers must go over, under, or through the hoop.

By changing the components of an activity, you can invent countless variations while creating conditions in which climbers can safely and confidently choose among interesting and relevant challenges. Participants will be more inclined to feel and act competent, connected, valuable, self-confident, and upbeat.

You probably already have access to valuable resources that make it easy to create variations for activities. For instance, chapter 7 offers climbing activities based on a theme of healthy living. You can find relevant ideas, games, and illustrations for variations on the activities in Physical Best and Fitnessgram (NASPE and AAHPERD's health-related fitness program), Jump Rope for Heart and Hoops for Heart (educational, fund-development programs that are cosponsored by the American Heart Association and AAHPERD), and MyPyramid, sponsored by the U.S. Department of Agriculture. Any one of these resources can provide many ideas. For instance, MyPyramid directs some of its information specifically to children ages 6 to 11, offering such activities as a Blast Off game, a coloring page, a worksheet, and other classroom materials that can be found on their Team Nutrition Web site (www.mypyramid.gov).

Similar resources exist for activities in other chapters. To create variations for the well-known games in chapter 3, look through your collection of board games and card games. Many of the math and number activities in chapter 4 are inspired by puzzles found in daily newspapers. And classroom teachers provided many ideas that led to the word and letter activities in chapter 5.

Add Excitement With Random Results

Several activities in chapters 3 through 7 use dice and spinners to guide the movements of climbers. You can use those items to identify which colored holds climbers must touch or avoid, the number of moves required to complete a sequence or solve a problem, and scores of other climbing options and decisions. For example, in Take-Away (chapter 6), climbers take turns subtracting available holds, creating a more difficult traversing route. In one variation of the activity, each hold is numbered 1 through 6, and a die roll specifies which holds can be subtracted. As another example, in Body Warp (chapter 3), a spinner points to the body part that the climber must move next and the color of hold that the climber must use.

15	9	5	16
7	14	3	4
11	6	1	12
2	10	8	13

FIGURE 1.16 You can throw beanbags at a large floor grid to determine random results.

Dice and spinners are readily available, but if you wish, you can determine random results by throwing beanbags onto a numbered grid (figure 1.16). Make the grid out of a large sheet of clear or light-colored vinyl or plastic, place it on the floor, and throw beanbags to determine the results.

A grid and beanbags can be used for integrating climbing with various academic skills. For instance, if a beanbag lands on the number 7, the climber must traverse the wall searching for a card that contains the Spanish word for seven (*siete*) or the Roman numeral for seven (VII). For a math challenge, toss two beanbags onto the grid and determine the sum of their numbers; the climber must make that many moves on the wall. For a travel challenge, the sum might determine how many locations the climber must visit while traversing.

Alternatively, you can make a grid out of a large piece of fabric on which a projected image has been traced, tape it to a wall, and throw ball darts to see where they stick. To make ball darts, tape strips of Velcro around tennis balls.

For a travel challenge, throw ball darts at a map or a grid marked with the names of locations (figure 1.17). Climbers must traverse to corresponding locations on the wall and identify something about them. If a ball dart hits the state of Colorado, the climber traverses to that label on the wall and must identify the state's capital, its major rivers or lakes, or a famous landmark.

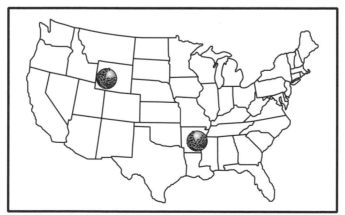

FIGURE 1.17 In travel activities, throw Velcro balls at a fabric map to determine a climber's next destination.

Setting Up Your Wall

Traverse-wall vendors often encourage increasing the level of difficulty by changing the position of the handholds. That's a reasonable suggestion, but many instructors find it impractical to keep rearranging handholds   especially when the climbers are kids, who usually vary greatly in size and ability. Although the level of difficulty is an important consideration, other kinds of adjustments can make a wall more or less challenging, not to mention more interesting and better suited to a greater variety of activities, such as those presented in this book.

Walls and holds come in all shapes and sizes (see the appendix for information on popular established vendors). You can buy large and small holds in various colors that are shaped as letters, numbers, or animals, for example. Walls can have a single color or many colors with a rocklike texture. Some walls even have magnetized panels and write-on, wipe-off surfaces. However, you don't need to purchase a huge collection of special equipment. You can prepare even the most basic wall for a variety of activities in simple, cost-effective ways. With a bit of foresight, a single preparation might suit several activities.

Creating Routes

There's no such thing as a typical climbing route. A good route is one that suits the abilities and interests of the participants. Holds that are too large, too small, too close together, too far apart, or inappropriately positioned can discourage success and enjoyment. Routes that are too demanding can dishearten even advanced climbers, and routes that are too monotonous or too easy also hold little appeal.

When placing holds to create a route, consider these guidelines:

- Install bottom footholds that provide a solid surface and are easy to stand on.

- Install holds in obvious locations (such as in a spot where a climber can easily put a hand on top of the hold) and in less obvious locations (such as in a spot that requires a sidepull or undercling).

- Ask participants of varying abilities to attempt traverses and look for potential trouble spots. You'll learn if any holds are too far apart, if the route is too easy or too hard, and so on.

- When creating several routes on a wall, distribute the challenges evenly. But also remember to vary the challenges within a single route, when possible.

- Properly identify routes by their level of difficulty. For example, use only red holds in a tricky route, or place red tape or stickers near the holds.
- Check the holds often. A common mistake is to overtighten holds, which can cause them to break or can weaken their anchor points. In the latter case, the anchor might break or come off the wall completely.

Coding Holds

Identifying the difficulty of a route is only one reason to label, or code, holds. Placing coded pieces of tape next to an assortment of holds will accommodate multiple activities. You can use marking tape made specifically for climbing walls or less expensive masking tape; some brands stick more firmly than others. Also consider whether you want to use plain tape or colored tape; colored tape can make the route more attractive.

Figure 1.18 shows an example of coding that uses standard masking tape. First, cut 52 small pieces of tape and write a different code on each piece. Each code involves some combination of colors, numbers, and letters. In all, each number (from 1 to 13) is used four times, each letter is used twice, and each color (red, blue, yellow, and green) is used 13 times. After writing all the codes, place the pieces of tape randomly next to holds, one piece per hold (figure 1.19).

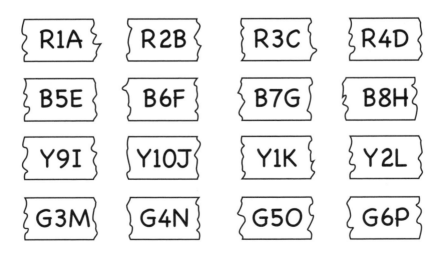

FIGURE 1.18 Write codes on separate pieces of masking tape. In this example, the first character is the color code (R = red, B = blue, Y = yellow, G = green), the second is the number, and the third is the letter.

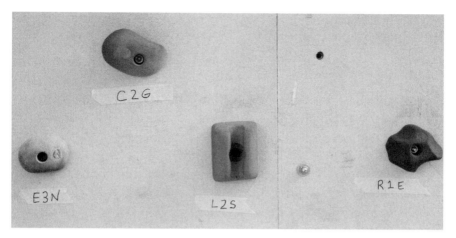

FIGURE 1.19 Place tape codes near holds to direct climbers during traversing activities.

Again, using the Add-On activity as an example, the colors, numbers, and letters can direct climbers in many ways. Consider these rule restrictions:

- If a climber's last move involved a yellow hold, the next move must use a hold of a different color.
- All green holds are off limits.
- If a climber's last move involved an even-numbered hold, the next move must use an odd-numbered hold.
- A climber's next move can't use a hold that has the same letter used in the previous move, or an adjacent letter. Thus, if the previous move involved a hold marked with the letter N, the next move can't use a hold marked with the letters M, N, or O.

Of course, many other coding schemes are possible. For example, on most walls, it's easy to slide playing cards behind the holds, and a single deck yields codes involving colors, suits, face cards, numbers, and jokers. However, the simple masking-tape scheme described previously works for many of the activities and variations in this book, and it requires little or no work rearranging handholds.

Sectioning the Wall

Instead of using tape to mark holds, you can use it to mark sections of the wall. Again, a few well-placed vertical or horizontal strips can make many activity variations possible. You can mark sections with straight strips of tape or with strips arranged in a zigzag pattern.

Vertical strips can mark wall sections to create climbing areas in which special instructions apply (figure 1.20). Here are some examples:

- Climbers can begin anywhere but must pass through three of the four sections.
- All climbers must remain either in sections A and B only or in sections C and D only.
- Each climber must select one section in which she'll use only three handholds.
- Team 1 must select a section in which no member of the team will use any green handholds.

It's easy to imagine the many challenges afforded by vertical sections. These kinds of columns work well in activities such as Q&A (chapter 3). Similarly, you can section the wall with horizontal strips of tape and create new climbing rules (figure 1.21). Here are some examples:

- Climbers must not place both feet above the bottom line.
- All traverses must use at least one handhold in every section.
- Each climber selects one of the lines near the center of the wall. Thereafter, the climber can use only handholds above the line and only footholds below the line.

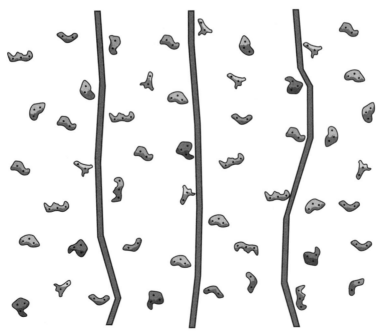

FIGURE 1.20 Use vertical strips of tape to make climbing columns.

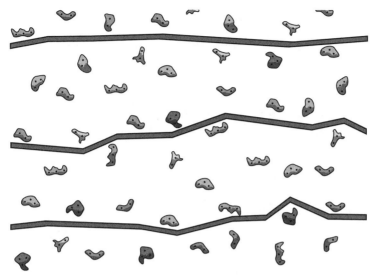

FIGURE 1.21 Use horizontal strips of tape to create climbing rows.

To diversify the challenges even further, you can combine vertical and horizontal strips of tape to create segmented columns. Simple grids can be used in an activity such as Connect the Dots (figure 1.22). Again, remember that the strips need not be symmetrical. In fact, by adding, removing, and rotating strips here and there, you can create triangles, trapezoids, and other more complex designs that open new possibilities (figure 1.23).

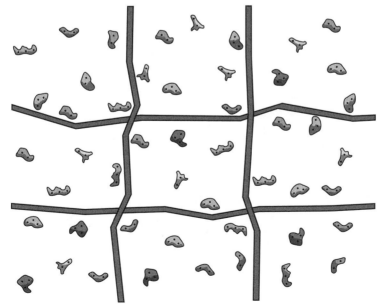

FIGURE 1.22 Combine strips to create a simple grid.

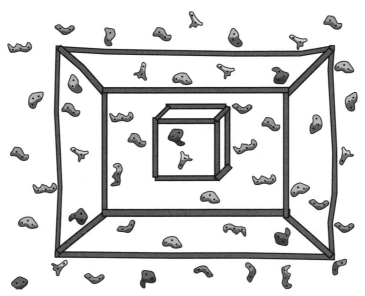

FIGURE 1.23 Use tape to create more complex wall patterns.

Mapping the Wall

You can use a photograph of your traverse wall and an overhead transparency of any illustration to turn the wall into a map. Although this idea is quite simple, it has great possibilities and variations.

Step 1

Take a photograph of your traverse wall. Photocopy the picture so that it fits on a standard 8.5-by-11-inch sheet of paper.

Step 2

Make an overhead transparency of a viable illustration. Figure 1.24 shows an example of a simple map of the United States, but you can find similar illustrations anywhere. Those old coloring books that you've stored away might soon come in handy.

FIGURE 1.24 Simple map of the United States.

Step 3

Lay the transparency over the copy of the wall photo, and make a photocopy of the two items combined. Voila! You have just created a map of your traverse wall (figure 1.25). Make copies of the map for climbers so they can orient themselves when traversing. Also, because the map is just a representation of what *could* appear on the wall, teach climbers how to interpret the map.

Imagine some of the possibilities. Using a map of the United States, students can identify and follow climbing routes from coast to coast. This might involve visiting or avoiding certain states, such as states whose names begin with M, states whose names repeat the same letter in succession (such as Mississippi), or states that repeat letters anywhere within their names (such as California). In addition, students might travel to the birthplace of the U.S. presidents in order or the home state of each team in a favorite professional sport.

Instead of creating a map of the United States, you can create a map of your state, the world, a golf course, the skeletal system, the nighttime sky, or any image that can direct climbers to various locations on the wall.

FIGURE 1.25 Superimpose a map or other illustration over a photo of your wall.

Summary

When instructors understand certain fundamentals of climbing, they can preserve the excitement of climbing while simultaneously reducing the risk of injury to participants. In this chapter, we covered general safety concerns that apply to all traversing activities. We discussed and gave examples of climbing terminology and techniques, followed by a few warm-up activities designed to prevent muscle and tendon injuries. Also included were suggestions for supervising a challenging yet safeguarded climbing environment. These included instructor and participant responsibilities. Finally, we recommended ways to modify activities and the climbing wall itself, all in an attempt to enthuse and engage the maximum number of participants in appropriate climbing experiences.

At this point you might be thinking, *Hey, these ideas are so obvious. Why didn't I think of them?* If so, you're on your way to saying, "Guess what I just created!" But before inventing new activities for your traverse wall or sampling the activities in chapters 3 through 7, we encourage you to think about what students will do when they're *not* on the wall. Just because some participants are not engaged in traversing, that doesn't mean they should simply stand around and watch. Indeed, you can lead them in activities and exercises that use their off-wall time very productively, as explained in chapter 2.

Lead-Up
Activities

When instructing students who have little or no climbing experience, you should begin with some basics. First of all, climbing should be fun. Initial success on a traverse wall can motivate someone from the start. However, an unsuccessful first climb might cause someone to decide against climbing again. This chapter offers activities that lead up to, but do not yet involve, climbing on the wall. Through various challenging and entertaining tasks on the ground, students learn foundational skills such as good communication, appropriate warm-ups, individual and group problem solving, and movements unique to climbing. Lead-up activities allow you to teach the principles while establishing a stimulating and motivating learning environment.

We begin this chapter with a discussion of dome cones, which introduce and accentuate climbing specifics such as learning to be an effective spotter, trying various climbing routes, working with partners and small groups, communicating effectively, and practicing balance and footwork technique. Activities with dome cones allow for a high student–teacher ratio, permit several students to be engaged at one time, afford maximum climbing time per student, and increase opportunities for you to observe, encourage, and evaluate.

Next, we present the Superstar Challenge activity, in which teams work toward climbing-related goals. All participants enhance their strength, endurance, and flexibility in a developmentally appropriate manner that is demanding but fun.

Finally, we offer a series of individual activities that support the basics of wall climbing. These tasks promote strength and balance and often involve the same kinds of problem solving and support that are required on the traverse wall. You can set up these activities as stations that precede climbing, or they can provide challenges for students waiting their turn on the wall.

Dome Cones

Dome cones, also referred to simply as domes, are small half-spheres (figure 2.1) that are placed in various patterns on the floor. Moving from dome to dome involves many of the movement and problem-solving challenges presented by the traverse wall. For example, both dome and climbing activities require footwork, balance, flexibility, self-confidence, concentration, communication, and teamwork. In other words, while using domes, students learn terms and movements that transfer directly to the traverse wall. Domes allow space for discovery and learning while presenting a safe opportunity for practicing the movements and skills for climbing.

Equipment

Dome activities require only minimal equipment, and there are several options for obtaining what you need. For instance, if you don't have a set of domes, you can

FIGURE 2.1 A standard set of dome cones.

use simple wooden blocks instead, which you can make inexpensively by cutting two-by-fours into separate pieces 4 to 8 inches (10 to 20 cm) long. Applying a nonskid surface to one side of each block will keep it from moving across the floor when stepped on. This is especially important on wood or tiled floors. Alternatively, instead of applying nonskid material to each block, you can spread out rolls of foam carpet pad and place the blocks on the flattened surface. Carpet pad is typically inexpensive, somewhat durable, easy to store, and easy to cut if necessary.

For the activities in this chapter, we suggest multiuse dome cones. These small domes, approximately 7 inches (18 cm) in diameter and 4 inches (10 cm) high, store easily and provide a consistent feel underfoot. Their durability depends on their rigidity. Many equipment providers furnish both soft and hard domes; opt for the hard version, which can support the weight of a 200-pound (91 kg) person. Domes are available in numerous bright colors, and you can order a set of 36 or 48 domes through most physical education equipment catalogs for approximately $50 to $80 U.S. (see the appendix).

Basic Dome Patterns

When placed in various patterns, dome cones present an assortment of challenges as students attempt to traverse them. Several of the activities in this chapter use either the rows formation or the pairs formation shown in figure 2.2.

You can alter the suggested space between domes to suit your students' needs and abilities and to support your program's goals. Generally, greater distances create greater challenges. Also, some of the off-wall activities, such as Single Rows and Rows Skipper, require that the domes be placed closer together.

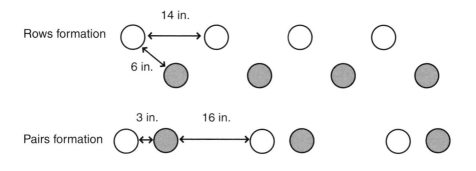

FIGURE 2.2 Rows and pairs formations.

Program Quality

Creating an effective climbing program is a challenge for any instructor. If students are to enjoy and benefit from climbing, they must be assured of developmentally appropriate activities, instructionally relevant practices that recognize their changing movement abilities, and attention to safety.

Activities and Practices

Proper use of dome cones supports a commitment to serving individual needs and abilities. Students can be challenged to try things at a level where they find personal success. You can adjust the number of domes, the distance between them, and the degree of assistance provided by spotters. For example, spotters can offer more physical help to accommodate children with severe balance deficits. Similarly, students who fall can be allowed to keep trying instead of being eliminated. Flexibility in learning experiences can create a high percentage of on-task engagement, suitable and motivating progressions, and a success-oriented environment for everyone.

Safety Policies

Just as you should do everything possible to offer a safe and encouraging climbing environment, you should do the same for dome activities. Even though domes are on the ground, their proper use demands a suitable margin of safety.

The general climbing protocols described in chapter 1 apply to movement from dome to dome as well. Remind students of the following guidelines:

- Always use at least two spotters (one on each side).
- Use slow, controlled movements. Don't let momentum carry you from dome to dome.
- Do not jump or leap from dome to dome.
- Don't rush or crowd the person in front of you.
- After completing each traverse, return to the line to be a spotter for the next person.

Spotting for domes also follows the general procedures outlined in chapter 1. It's good practice for spotting climbers on the wall, so be sure to reinforce proper stance, effective communication, cushioning rather than catching, and other aspects of good spotting.

Activities for Dome Cones

The introductory activities in this section emphasize basic movements that students can use later during more difficult dome cone challenges. To maximize participation, create five or six stations, each consisting of 10 to 12 domes arranged in the rows formation. To increase the challenge for each activity, domes can be arranged in pairs formation (see figure 2.2 on page 31). This configuration works well for many activities, yet some may require a different number of domes. At each station, one student traverses the domes while the others serve as spotters. The traversing student is called the climber even though the domes are on the floor. Before beginning each traverse, the climber and the spotters must engage in the proper communication sequence (see the following section). Once the climber steps onto the mat or completes the traverse, the next climber can begin the communication sequence.

Individual Activities

The following activities build on individual abilities and techniques. They reinforce skills such as weight shift, deliberate foot placement, controlled momentum, and concentration. In addition, the students practice appropriate communication and learn the essentials of good spotting. The movements in the last three activities (Rows Pick-Up, Rows Pick-Up Variations, and Single Rows) most closely resemble the movements used in climbing, which require students to shift their weight to find their center of gravity when reaching for objects.

Wobbly Walk

The point of this activity is teacher demonstration of how to travel, accompanied by how to spot correctly. Arrange dome cones about 6 inches (15 cm) apart in a rows formation (see figure 2.2 on page 31). Spotters stand along each side of the domes in proper position—feet apart and staggered, knees bent, and hands out with elbows bent. Before allowing the students to traverse, demonstrate the proper way to move across the domes. As you traverse, fall sideways, forward, and backward to check that students can demonstrate proper spotting technique.

Trust Walk

The point of this activity is teacher evaluation of proper spotting when a student traverses the domes. Use the same dome arrangement as in Wobbly Walk. Students stand in a spotting position along each side of the line. One student traverses the domes slowly as the group provides proper spotting. This activity allows you to assess the students' spotting skills and trustworthiness. Remind students that they are charged with building trust, not testing it.

Rows

Each climber walks from dome to dome with the right foot on the right row and the left foot on the left row (figure 2.3). This activity is no longer demonstration (Wobbly Walk) or assessment (Trust Walk)—now all six stations are operating independently and simultaneously.

FIGURE 2.3
A student walks the domes with one foot on each row.

Rows Crosser

When traversing, the climber steps across to the left row with the right foot (figure 2.4). This requires facing the direction of travel but turning the hips before proceeding to the next dome.

FIGURE 2.4
A student walks the domes by crossing her feet from row to row.

Backward Rows

Climbers perform the standard Rows activity while moving backward.

Rows Squatter

Climbers walk from dome to dome in the rows formation while in a squat position.

Rows Skipper

Decrease the distance between the domes in the rows formation. By stretching their legs way out, climbers try to skip one dome, then two domes, and so on until reaching their maximum distance.

Blindfolded Rows

Climbers traverse the domes in the rows formation while blindfolded.

Rows Pick-Up

The climber takes two steps and squats to pick up a beanbag that is lying between two domes (figure 2.5). Then the climber moves two more spaces, squats, and picks up a second beanbag, leaving the first beanbag in the spot where the second was found. The climber continues to exchange beanbags while traversing the domes.

FIGURE 2.5
A student pauses while walking the domes to pick up a beanbag.

Rows Pick-Up Variation

In this variation, beanbags lie in various locations around the perimeter of the traverse. As in Rows Pick-Up, climbers move, squat, and pick up beanbags, exchanging them down the line. Distances between the beanbags vary, so climbers must situate their bodies in various balanced positions before reaching out to pick up the objects.

Single Rows

Set up domes for Rows Skipper and place beanbags in the middle of the two sets of domes. The climber puts one foot onto the first dome (thus shifting weight to that foot), crouches, picks up the beanbag, stands, and then steps with the trailing foot onto another dome. As with Rows Pick-Up, the climber picks up and replaces each new beanbag while traversing.

Cooperative Team Activities

You can also use dome cones to create cooperative group initiatives. Two examples, Domes Add-On and Team Square, appear in this section. In these and other team initiatives, the students build on the basic skills they learned in previous individual challenges.

Domes Add-On

Place dome cones randomly inside a 10-foot (3 m) square. This game, similar to Follow the Leader, imitates the Add-On activity played on the traverse wall.

Four or five students can work together as a group. The first student to enter the square steps on four dome cones, one at a time. The other group members watch and try to remember the sequence. Then a second student repeats the first four moves and adds one or two more. Next, a third student repeats all previous moves and adds one or two more. The sequence continues until everyone has added one or two moves, at which point the group is awarded the letter C.

The group then starts over with a different member stepping on four dome cones to create a new sequence. If everyone negotiates the subsequent traverse, the group is awarded the letter L. The goal is to complete five sequences and spell the word *climb*.

You can also present each group with a card that explains the task and imposes some kind of rule or restriction, such as "No one may touch any yellow domes." Alternatively, you can give each group a different card with a unique restriction, such as the following:

- No one may touch any green domes.
- No one may touch any blue or red domes.

- The first climber must touch at least two yellow domes. After that, no climber may touch any yellow domes.

To make this activity more of a competition among groups, change the goal. Instead of earning letters by completing sequences, climbers earn a letter each time they fail to do so. Any group that spells the word *domes* is eliminated. Again, you can make the activity more difficult by imposing additional rules or restrictions.

In both versions, you can also make the activity longer or shorter by changing the word that is spelled to *top, traverse,* or anything else you choose.

Team Square

This group challenge is similar to Domes Add-On but more difficult. Place dome cones in a 10-foot (3 m) square so as to create four paths that cross one another (figure 2.6). Each path begins on a different side of the square and is represented by color—one is made of red domes, one is made of blue domes, and so on. Set up at least two paths so that they can't be crossed without help. In other words, part of the route might require a spotter because climbers have to attempt a considerable stretch to move between certain domes. However, don't reveal this fact to the class. Simply assign each group a specific color, and tell the students to cross the area by stepping only on domes of that color (and without touching the ground).

Depending on the group, the challenge can be either a competitive or a cooperative event. After completing the first round, you might add a rule that each team must traverse every colored path.

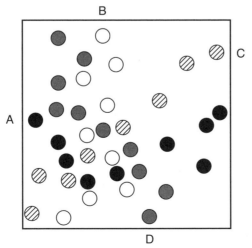

FIGURE 2.6 In Team Square, four kinds of domes create four paths that cross one another.

Variations

As with the traversing activities in this book, you can create many variations for dome activities. Consider any of the following possibilities.

Twist and Turn

A climber must place a hand or foot on a designated color, perhaps determined by the roll of a die. The next roll determines the color on which another foot or hand must be placed, until both hands and both feet are on colored domes. More rolls of the die determine subsequent moves, and the player continues until unable to complete a move or until successfully traversing the entire square. This can be played simultaneously with two or more climbers.

Checkers

Two teams face each other on opposite sides of a square or rectangle. The goal is for a team to get to the other side first. If a team member commits a fault (steps onto the floor, steps backward, or interferes with an opposing team's player), that player must start over. Increase the difficulty by placing five numbered beanbags randomly throughout the square. Each team member must pick up a beanbag in its numerical sequence.

Golf

On a piece of paper, teams of three chart nine courses. Each climber has three holes, a par 3, par 4, and par 5, for a total of nine holes per team. The par of the hole is the number of domes that must be touched from the designated tee to the flag (for example, par 3 requires touching 3 yellow domes).

Floor Obstacle Course

Climbers must negotiate obstacles (such as hoops, basketballs, short hurdles) that have been placed among the domes. They must climb above or below, depending on the height of the obstacles. If you combine this with the previous golf variation, the obstacles could be hazards on the golf course.

Miscellaneous Variations

- Lay out domes in the shape of a square or rectangle. Teams draw maps with routes that other teams must follow.
- Climbers retrieve numbered beanbags while crossing domes and try to reach a specific total (such as 12).
- Climbers retrieve lettered beanbags while crossing domes and try to spell a particular word (such as the climber's name).
- Climbers retrieve lettered beanbags and try to spell a word that is suggested by a clue. For example, "Using the side of the foot to stand on small, flat holds is called _____" (*edging*).
- Carry an object (ball, cup of Styrofoam pellets, marbles) from one location to another without dropping or spilling the contents; or

carry the object without using the hands (such as a beanbag on the shoulder or head).

- Climbers cannot step onto the same color twice in succession.
- Traverse the square using only a predetermined number of domes.
- Traverse with a partner; both partners must remain on domes and cannot share a dome.
- Pick up a beanbag and toss to a partner who is standing outside the square; pick up a second beanbag, again tossing to partner. Replace the second with the first after partner tosses the first one back. As a variation, the climber cannot pick up the same color twice in succession; or the partner is also moving among domes.
- Teams travel among domes. Each time the first person retrieves an object, it must be passed to all other teammates and returned before the first person can continue moving.

Approximating Wall Activities

Many dome activities can be modified to approximate those performed on the traverse wall. For example, make slight changes to Twist and Turn, and it becomes the wall activity Body Warp (chapter 3). Also in chapter 3 is Memory, a game in which holds are marked with picture cards, and climbers earn points for each matching pair found. You can use cards in a similar fashion with dome cones.

Superstar Challenge

Beginning climbers feel that strength and endurance are their major weaknesses. Another element of fitness that is important for climbers is flexibility. Teams work together to collect points indicating various levels of achievement. Holds are differentiated somehow (by color, size, or shape); ribbons, certificates, wall charts, or other small awards acknowledge completion at various levels of challenge.

To increase strength, endurance, and flexibility, create teams, each of which can accumulate points by completing strength and conditioning exercises related to climbing. Thus, teams (not individuals) attempt to reach various levels of achievement. Teams can also attempt to gain points during recess or before or after school. This might require adult volunteer supervision and recording and a simple and accurate method of record keeping. The goals are for students to work together, to exercise on their own, and to encourage more parental involvement.

Each student has a 3-by-5 index card with the student's name, team name, activity (such as push-ups), and numbers of correct repetitions necessary for completing a card (figure 2.7). Activities can incorporate

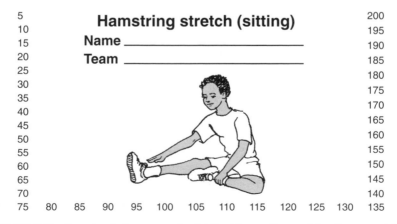

FIGURE 2.7 Sample challenge cards: (a) Bent-knee sit-ups, (b) pull-ups, and (c) hamstring stretch.

the traverse wall, but a wall isn't necessary. Exercises such as push-ups, sit-ups, and stretches can be performed almost anywhere. With the benefit of some playground equipment or weights, you can incorporate pull-ups, dips, wrist and arm curls, calf raises, and the like.

During recess (or whenever the program occurs), students check out their individual Climbing Team cards and a parent volunteer observes them to verify that they correctly perform their chosen activity (for example, sit-ups). To expedite the process, each student gets no more than one minute. If the student performs the task properly, the adult recorder punches (using a small hole puncher) the student's card indicating the number of correct repetitions. When a team gains a certain number of points (such as 2,000) or completes a certain number of cards (such as two for each teammate), their punched-out cards are laminated and placed on a Climbing Team Hall of Fame board, which is prominently displayed for the entire year. Teams acquiring many points (such as 10,000) or completing many cards (for example, all team-mates complete all cards, or all teammates complete at least 2 of 5, and at least 3 complete all 5) might receive a special acknowledgment.

Strength and Balance

Climbing must be kept in perspective. It is different from many other physical endeavors where winning and losing are intrinsic to the activity. Certainly climbing can involve competition, but "climbing is a very internal activity, and most kids will judge themselves on their own merits, not on how they compare with others in the gym" (Hurni, 2003, p. 4). Since two key ingredients for successful climbing are strength and balance, you can provide individualized activities that enhance both.

By capitalizing on the existing abilities of each climber and using simple equipment and body weight, you can help climbers develop strength and balance before they ever attempt to traverse a wall. Some of these activities provide the resistance necessary for building enough strength to support the body during climbing, while others help participants maintain or regain balance. Some of the activities focus on either strength or balance in isolation, whereas others combine the two. Most of the activities call for equipment that is readily available in most physical education catalogs (see the appendix) or at your local discount store.

All of the activities can be presented at stations. We prefer the use of stations, among which students may rotate according to their interests and needs. Children may have varying degrees of success with these stations, and in the beginning it is a good idea to convey that each will be challenging in different ways for each person. Several stations may require the support of a partner. Also, once wall climbing begins, those students who are waiting their turn on the traverse wall can use the stations. You can instruct students to engage in a predetermined number of off-wall stations before rotating to the climbing wall for a repeat climb, and task sheets can guide students in addressing a variety of specific strength- and balance-development tasks.

Strength

There is no doubt that climbing requires strength. Pushing with the legs requires lower-body strength, and pulling and pushing with the arms requires upper-body strength. Core strength is just as important for successful traverse climbing. Core strength is the development of muscles of the back and abdomen surrounding the core area of the body. These bands of muscles, which run in various directions around the body, provide the core with a strong support structure. This structure absorbs shock when jumping and landing and stabilizes the body when moving through space. To maximize success while climbing on the wall, students should develop core strength while on stable ground.

It is not the intent of this book to provide an in-depth look at training techniques and physical conditioning for climbers. For those interested in advanced knowledge about various types of training and schedules, we recommend Michelle Hurni's *Coaching Climbing* (2003).

There are two types of muscle fibers. Slow-twitch fibers control endurance, and fast-twitch fibers control strength. Less resistance with many repetitions increases endurance strength (e.g., can lift 20 pounds 10 times before tiring); more resistance with fewer repetitions enhances explosive strength (e.g., can lift 250 pounds one time). To ensure the best all-around development, climbers must vary the resistance and the number of times they would lift, push, or pull a given weight. Another element of fitness that is important for climbers is flexibility, which is covered in chapter 1. Strength without flexibility leads to short, stiff muscle fibers. Thus, the following strength activities should be interspersed with stretching.

Lead-Lead, Follow-Follow

The concept of leading and following is an important first step in climbing. Students need to plan moves in which they lead with the hand and foot on the same side and then follow with the other hand and foot. Though it sounds easy, this can be a major challenge, especially for young children. But even older children who are unfamiliar with climbing sometimes struggle with planning before moving. For children who cannot remember to lead with one side and then follow with the other, getting stuck on the wall with nowhere to go is frustrating and confusing.

For young climbers and as an introduction to this concept, consider the analogy of the engine and caboose. When climbing, the lead side is the engine, and the following side is the caboose. Once the engine sets out on a journey, it must take the caboose along as it travels. Students initially need to be reminded that they must consistently lead (hand), lead (foot), follow (hand or foot), follow (hand or foot).

An activity that reinforces the concept of lead and follow involves leading with one side while moving across the gym from one poly spot to the next using just the feet. Students traverse a course of poly spots laid out in a straight line across the room. They begin by moving from right to left across the entire room and then from left to right. Leading in both directions while traversing the poly spots helps students learn this pattern of feet.

Since climbing involves the hands and feet, the next challenge is to coordinate both. One way to accomplish this is to crouch down on all fours and navigate a double row of poly spots. Make sure that when, say, the right foot moves forward, the right hand follows before moving the left foot. Initially, students may require the assistance of a training partner to remember to navigate the spots using the lead-lead, follow-follow patterning. If a student is having difficulty with this concept, a partner can repeat, "Lead-lead, follow-follow," throughout the sequence.

The same practice activity can be accomplished using a double agility ladder or linear double grid taped to the floor (figure 2.8). Such ladders are available from many vendor catalogs under the categories of fitness or agility; see the appendix for some recommended vendors.

FIGURE 2.8 A student uses a double agility ladder to practice lead-lead, follow-follow.

Students navigate across the double grid on their hands and feet, as if in a push-up position, remembering to pattern their movements so that they move laterally, using hand-foot with the lead side and hand-foot with the follow side. Though it sounds simple, maintaining this movement pattern while holding the body off the ground in a push-up position mimics climbing but without the added possibility of falling. Students develop upper-body, lower-body, and core strength while practicing this drill.

Hover

Some of the best core exercises borrowed from Pilates can easily be used with children. One challenging exercise is the hover. To get into this position, lie prone (facedown), placing your elbows on the floor next to the shoulders. Next, create an inverted V with your hands to elbows, resting them atop one another in a relaxed position on the floor. Pull the body into a straight position off the floor, much like a push-up, with the abdominal muscles pulled in toward the spine and the body aligned in a tight position. The body is supported on the forearms and two feet (figure 2.9a).

Focus on the abdominal muscles, control the breathing, and hold. Initially students may only be able to hold this position for 10 to 20 seconds, eventually working up to 30-second and 60-second intervals.

This exercise works the entire abdominal area, back, and shoulders. For participants whose core muscles are too strained by this activity, the lower body can be supported on two knees, much like a modified push-up (figure 2.9b).

Superman

This is another excellent exercise that strengthens and stretches the core. Lie on the floor in a prone position with arms outstretched in front of you and the legs extended back. Squeeze the buttocks and lift the arms, shoulders, and legs off the floor simultaneously, much like Superman flying (figure 2.10). Start with 10-second then 20-second and 30-second intervals, remembering to control breathing and relaxing as much as possible while holding this position.

Physio Ball

All students can benefit by using physio balls with specific execution assignments for the development of abdominal, back, and core strength (figure 2.11). You can use this versatile piece of equipment for beginner push-ups and crunches, supine glute bridges, and Y holds; then you can move on to more advanced extension activities using light weights.

a

b

FIGURE 2.9 Students can do the hover exercise with their knees (a) off the ground or (b) on the ground.

FIGURE 2.10 Remind students to breathe and relax while holding the Superman position.

FIGURE 2.11 Students can use a physio ball to practice push-ups and more.

Aerobic Steps

Step activities have long been used for the development of lower-body strength. The step is a versatile piece to include in a circuit of lower-body fitness development stations. The step is made of plastic and is usually topped with a rubber nonskid surface. For more of a challenge in aerobic exercises, the height of the step can be adjusted by adding more steps (layers).

Jump Flags

Students practice explosive strength by jumping as high as possible to touch flags that are suspended from basketball baskets, the ceiling, or other heights.

Top 10 Upper Body Fitness Center

This all-inclusive station provides children with 10 challenging applications of upper-body fitness development and can be used as a stand-alone station to develop upper-body strength while still maintaining fun. It is not one piece of equipment, but rather a collection of different items that combine to create 10 challenges. Various equipment vendors offer the Top 10 Upper Body Fitness Center (see the appendix).

Resistance Training

Students can perform basic weight-training exercises using lightweight dumbbells (1 pound or .5 kg), exercise tubing, rubber exercise bands, medicine balls, weighted yoga balls, lightweight gel balls, or sand cuff weights. Most manufacturers provide suggested activities for their equipment. These can be incorporated into several fun stations that accommodate the abilities of various age groups. For example, using cuff weights, students can begin by lying on their backs, knees slightly bent, straightening one leg at a time and bending it back to rest on the floor. The degree of difficulty can be increased in several ways:

- Repeat several times with the same leg and then the other leg
- Instead of lying on the back, sit leaning back on the elbows and, holding a basketball or medicine ball between the ankles, lift both legs
- Trace small circles in the air with both feet
- Repeat with larger circles or write your name in the air (or your school, numbers from 1 to 10, and so on)
- Repeat with added weight
- Repeat but with straight arms supporting the body in the back

Balance

Climbing demands balance, which means that the center of gravity, although constantly shifting, is squarely over the feet. When climbing, moving the center of gravity from where it should be not only can hinder progress but can also lead to increased strain on the fingers. This occurs when a climber leans so far that the weight is shifted from the legs and feet to the arms and fingers. Correct body posture is therefore important and can be practiced at various stations. Because of the instability of equipment used in many of the following activities, consider using spotters and pay attention to safety. General guidelines for spotting appear in chapter 1; review and enforce those guidelines with students for these balancing activities.

Foam Core Balance

Cut a 6-inch-thick (about 15 cm) foam core or swim noodle in half through the middle so that one side is round and one side is flat. Turn the core cut side down to the ground. Students balance on the core with the balls of the feet as a base. They maintain balance for 30 seconds, working to elongate the body upward and stabilizing the core area. Direct them to repeat this for several sets.

Now turn the core so that it is curved side down. Students attempt the same balance with this new core position. If you have sufficient half cores, these can be set up as two separate stations.

This same balance concept can be executed using the following equipment with varying challenge involved:

- Flat noodle
- Full core
- Balance beam

- Inflatable stability pad
- Balance boards of assorted heights
- BOSU ball (an acronym for "both sides up," BOSU balls, also called BOSU balance trainers, are inflatable, dome-shaped balls that are about 1 foot high [30 cm] and 2 feet [60 cm] in diameter; they may be used curved side up or curved side down)

Seesaw Balance Board

These types of balance boards are generally higher than the wooden-type balance boards that have a short elevation built into the center of a board, thus creating a great balance challenge (figure 2.12).

Woggler Walk

Students attempt to balance and walk using a woggler, which looks something like a skateboard with large, nonskid pads (instead of wheels) at each end (figure 2.13). This piece of equipment requires students to maintain balance while shifting weight from one foot to the other in order to walk across a floor.

A more advanced challenge is to move across a space backward on a woggler, then attempt to walk through a prescribed woggler course.

FIGURE 2.12 It can be challenging to keep your balance on a seesaw board.

Bouncing Board

The students maintain balance while gripping a bouncing board or platform ball with their feet and advancing across the floor (figure 2.14).

Duck Walker

This piece of equipment is a balance board that rocks and spins 360 degrees to allow students to navigate across the room while on their feet (figure 2.15). It can also improve arm and shoulder strength by placing the hands on the flat end panels.

FIGURE 2.13 A student on a woggler must shift her weight to move from ring to ring.

FIGURE 2.14 Use your feet to grip a bouncing platform ball while you move across the floor.

FIGURE 2.15   A student on a duck walker can rock and spin to cross the floor.

Stepping or Balance Blocks

This activity involves blocks that can be used in several ways. Students begin this challenge by stepping across blocks that are placed with the flat side down. As their skill progresses, they can step on blocks that are placed with the round side down. Finally, students can use rope handles and walk on the blocks as stilts (first with the flat side down and then with the round side down).

Balance-Board Maze

Students balance on a low balance board while trying to navigate a small ball through a grooved maze course around the surface of the balance board. This activity challenges students not only to maintain their balance but also to focus on a second task at the same time, much as wall climbing does.

Summary

Activities in this chapter promote skills and abilities that will transfer to the climbing wall. One aim is to improve strength and balance, both of which are necessary for using the forces that carry a climber from one position to the next. Another is to draw attention to good climbing practices. These include responsibilities for both climber and spotter and protocols for communication and mutual support. Finally, the activities can engage participants in a variety of challenging and innovative activities that will lead to increased success and enthusiasm among all young climbers.

Well-Known Games

3

Just as there are many variants of familiar card games (such as poker, rummy, and solitaire), the activities in this chapter are variations of memorable games enjoyed during childhood. In some games, such as Memory (a popular game in which cards are placed facedown and players attempt to uncover matching pairs), many seven-year-olds can beat their parents, despite their best efforts. Although the activities in this chapter are easy to understand, they can present challenges to children and adults alike.

Simon Says

Overview

Similar to the childhood game of Simon Says, one student designated as Simon instructs the class on which climbing moves to make.

Setup

No additional equipment is required.

Description

This activity begins when a designated leader (Simon) gives a group of climbers 10 to 15 seconds to get on the wall using all four points of contact (both hands and both feet). After the climbers are in place, Simon calls out various commands, such as, "Simon says, move your right hand to a lower handhold," and the climbers do their best to comply.

Climbers are eliminated if they make a move that isn't prefaced with "Simon says" or if they are unable to make a legitimately requested move.

Variations

- Simon can instruct climbers to use a specific grip (such as a pinch grip, an undercling, a sidepull, and so on).
- Simon can instruct climbers to move to a specific color (for example, climbers must move to a red hold).
- Simon can instruct climbers in a very specific manner (for example, "Simon says, climbers must move the left hand to a blue handhold below and to the right and move the right foot to a green foothold up and to the left).
- Letters or numbers can be placed next to the handholds, whereby Simon instructs the climbers to move to the letters or numbers.
- If a player is "out," that player changes roles with Simon.

Body Warp

Overview

Climbers must touch holds of specific colors.

Setup

Use a color-coded spinner wheel (many students like to construct these as an off-wall activity) and like-colored spots near holds.

Description

This activity was inspired by a common childhood game and begins with climbers spread out across the traverse wall (climbers should not begin above or below another climber). The caller—a student using the spinner wheel—instructs the climbers where to place their hands and feet. For example, if the wheel points to "right foot red," the caller tells climbers to move their right foot to a red hold. As another example, a certain move might require that all climbers place their right foot on a hold that is shaped like an animal (as shown in the photo). A climber is out when a move cannot be made.

Variations

- The caller can use a set of dice instead of a color-coded spinner. On the first die rolled, numbers correspond to colors (1 is red, 2 is blue, 3 is green, 4 is orange, 5 is yellow, and 6 is climber's choice). On the second die rolled, numbers correspond to body parts (1 is right foot, 2 is left foot, 3 is right hand, 4 is left hand, and 5 and 6 are either hand). Therefore, rolls of 1 and 4 mean that the left hand must move to a red hold).

- When rolling dice, choose two students to be callers. One rolls the first die and the other rolls the second die.

- Climbers begin in their own personal space and are out when they make contact with another climber.

- The activity can be played in many groups consisting of two climbers and two callers; roles are switched when climbers are unable to make the next move or contact another climber.
- Climbers can begin standing on the floor, facing the traverse wall. For example, if the caller says "right foot red" and the climber cannot step on a red hold even when starting on the floor, then they would switch roles. This variation often results in frequent switching of roles.
- Instead of using a spinner or dice, a caller instructs the class based on her choice. In other words, the caller simply gives instructions such as this: "Right foot red, left hand green, right hand blue." Change callers at designated times. Encourage callers to be thoughtful; the goal is to see how long the climbers can remain on the wall, not to knock them off quickly with impossible directions.
- In a hat, place small pieces of paper with climbing moves written on them (such as right foot red, left hand blue). The caller pulls one out, reads the move to the climbers, and places the paper back into the hat.

Memory

Overview

While traversing, climbers seek matching cards.

Setup

Use masking tape, double-sided Velcro tape, and 20 pairs of matching picture cards (such as pairs of animals, trees, automobiles) placed randomly next to handholds, with the picture sides facing the wall.

Description

This activity is similar to the card game and TV show requiring concentration and recall. It begins with a climber traversing the wall and turning over any one card. The climber places the card on the wall facing out for the entire group to view while he traverses to another card. The climber turns a second card facing out for the entire group to view. If the second card matches the first one, the climber collects that pair and goes again. If it is not a match, the climber must turn both cards back to facing the wall, and the next climber takes a turn. The climber with the most pairs wins.

Variations

- A player's turn ends after that person turns over any two cards, regardless of making a match.
- Vertically divide the traverse wall into two or three sections, allowing more than one game to be played at once.
- Increase or decrease the number of matching pairs to change the level of memory challenge.
- Memory matching cards can have numbers or words instead of pictures.
- Memory matching cards can have pictures of adult and baby animals; a climber must match the adult with the baby.
- Memory matching cards can be designed so that climbers must match similar things or opposite things (such as *hot* matched with *cold*).

- Words can be written in Spanish on one card and matched to English on the other.
- Play the game with small-sided teams.
- Turns end when a climber falls off the wall.
- Include wild cards to make a pair with any other card.
- The climber turns over a card on the wall, and a player who is not on the wall must locate a matching card from cards placed on the floor.

Connect the Dots

Overview

This is similar to games such as Tic-Tac-Toe and Checkers. Climbers take turns placing markers while trying to get four in a row horizontally, vertically, or diagonally.

Setup

Use red dots, black dots, and masking tape. Masking tape divides the wall into a six-row by eight-column grid. Any given box might contain more than one climbing hold.

Description

Players begin by choosing who will be the red dots and who will be the black dots. Red dots go first. The first climber traverses to any hold on the wall and places one of her dots next to it. The second climber may traverse to any other hold on the wall, placing one of his dots next to it. Only one hold per box may have a dot placed next to it. The first player to connect four of her dots in a row horizontally, vertically, or diagonally in adjacent boxes wins.

Variations

- Climber 1 makes three climbing moves; climber 2 must follow those moves. If climber 2 cannot copy the sequence, climber 1 places a dot next to the final hold in the move. If climber 2 can copy the sequence, he places a dot next to the final hold. Climber 2 then sets three climbing moves for climber 1 to follow. This continues until one climber connects four dots in a row horizontally, vertically, or diagonally in adjacent boxes.

- Teams of three or four may play, and the playing order can enhance team strategies. Teams must agree on the most effective order for climbing. For instance, imagine two teams of four climbers each. With 48 spaces, after one rotation of each team, only 40 spaces will remain. Each subsequent rotation leaves fewer spaces, and those remaining spaces might be the most difficult. A possible team strategy could be to avoid having the less able climber go last in a team's rotation, since that climber might not be capable of traversing to one of the remaining open spots.

- Climber 1 makes four climbing moves. Climber 2 must follow those moves. If climber 2 falls, then he must place a dot next to the last hold touched. If climber 2 does not fall, no dots are placed on the wall and the playing order switches. The first climber to connect four dots in a row horizontally, vertically, or diagonally in adjacent boxes loses.
- Increase or decrease the number of columns and rows to change the size of the playing area.
- Increase or decrease the number of dots required in a row to win.
- Divide the wall into two equal playing areas to allow two games to be played at once.

Q&A

Overview

A climber traverses the wall and reads a Q&A answer, or clue, taped next to a hold. Other group members attempt to respond by identifying the question that would elicit such a clue.

Setup

Using masking tape, divide the traverse wall vertically into four or five Q&A categories. At the top of the wall, tape category names written on paper. Under their corresponding categories, tape small index cards with point values from 100 to 500 written on one side and Q&A clues written on the other side. Point values should be facing out. Higher point values are taped to higher holds, and lower point values are taped to lower holds. You'll also need an answer key for the game-show host, score cards for each team, markers, and bells, horns, clickers, clackers, whistles, or kazoos for "buzzing" in the answers.

Description

This activity is designed for small groups. A climber is chosen at random and begins the game by traversing to any handhold that has a Q&A point value taped below it. While still on the wall, the climber reads the Q&A clue out loud to all remaining players. The first team to buzz in gets 3 seconds to answer in the form of a question. For example, in the category of animals, the clue might be "Furry and lays eggs." A correct response would be "What is a platypus?" If the team gives an incorrect answer, they lose the point value on the card and all remaining teams have an opportunity to answer. If no team provides a correct response after buzzing in, the climber remains on the wall and gets to pick another Q&A clue. However, if a team provides a correct response, they collect the point value and take control of the board by having one of their players replace the former climber. Climbers are not allowed to answer questions while on the wall. The team with the most points after all clues are read wins the game.

Variations

- Instructors, cooperating teachers, or students in earlier classes can write the Q&A clues.
- Ideas for categories are anagrams, state capitals, famous pop icons, sports figures, biology, chemistry, and health-related topics.
- To encourage more climbing, climbers must enter the wall from a specified area and traverse to the center of the wall before they can begin traversing to a Q&A clue card.
- All Q&A clues that are unanswered can be recycled for future games. Students are encouraged to remember what the clues were in order to find the correct answer outside of the classroom.

Go Fish

Overview

Climbers traverse the wall and retrieve cards ("go fishing"), attempting to find matching pairs.

Setup

You'll need a deck of 52 cards. Place cards next to various holds; conceal the numbers and suits.

Description

This activity is designed for pairs. To begin, each climber traverses the wall retrieving five cards of her choice to create a playing hand (one student climbs while the other spots). Cards may be tucked in the waistband or placed in a pocket. Climbers should not show their cards to one another. After retrieving a five-card playing hand, they step off the wall and then check to see if they have any matching pairs. (For example, climber 1 retrieves the following five cards: 3 of diamonds, ace of spades, 3 of hearts, 10 of spades, and jack of clubs; therefore, the 3 of diamonds and 3 of hearts are one matching pair.)

Taking turns, climbers ask one another for cards to help create matching pairs (using the remaining hand from the previous example, climber 1 would ask climber 2 if he had a 10, jack, or an ace). If climber 2 did have the card that climber 1 asked for, climber 1 gets the card and has one more matching pair. If climber 2 did not have the card climber 1 asked for, climber 2 would instruct climber 1, "Go fish." When a climber "goes fishing," she traverses the wall and retrieves one additional card to add to her hand. The climber with the most matching pairs when the first player runs out of cards wins.

Variations

- Use the same setup as the Memory game described previously (for example, pairs of animals, trees, automobiles).
- Divide the wall into three vertical sections with masking tape, thereby allowing three games to be played at the same time.
- Use one or two sections for Go Fish while playing a different game, such as Memory, in the remaining section.
- Increase the number of cards used (that is, use two decks of cards).
- Divide the wall into three diagonal sections (see pages 23-25 for various ways to section a wall) to provide various levels of challenge for climbers.
- As a way to add new strategies, use Memory and playing cards during the same game.

Add-On

Overview

Climbers follow another climber's route and then add moves to that route.

Setup

No additional equipment is required.

Description

Two or more climbers can do this activity. The activity begins when all climbers agree on a beginning sequence of three climbing moves. The first climber starts traversing using those moves and finishes the turn by adding one more climbing move to the sequence. Each subsequent player follows the previous route and finishes by adding one more climbing move to the route. Climbers continue in the climbing rotation until they cannot complete the sequence. The final climber who is able to continue adding to the sequence wins.

Variations

- Climbers must follow an exact sequence (for example, begin with right foot on red hold, left foot on green hold, right hand on small pinch grip, and left hand underclinging the blue hold).
- Climbers are allowed to use any footholds but must follow a prescribed sequence of handholds.
- Off-wall climbers (such as a spotter) can assist by reminding the climber where to go, or they are not allowed to coach at all.
- Climbers must add to the sequence as requested by the off-wall climbers (for example, off-wall climbers may request that the climber add on by moving up, down, left, or right).
- Begin by splitting the class into teams of three or four and allow each team to play Add-On within their small groups for 10 minutes. During those 10 minutes, each team must record their progress on paper. After 10 minutes, teams swap routes and have a chance to practice.
- Set up the previously described game so that all of the team routes are combined as one final route.
- Combine with the activity Pointer in chapter 6, in which a pointer determines the next move to be added on.

Horse

Overview

This is an adaptation of the basketball elimination game. In sequence, climbers attempt to copy the movements of the first climber.

Setup

No additional equipment is required.

Description

This activity is designed for small groups. In a predetermined sequence, climbers attempt to copy the movements of the first climber. The first climber makes a series of traversing movements. The second climber attempts to copy those movements. If the second climber is unsuccessful, the letter H is awarded. This process is followed until all group members attempt the first climber's movements. Any subsequent group members failing to copy the first climber's movements also acquire the letter H. Round 2 begins with a new lead climber.

The game ends when a climber spells *horse*. Similar to the basketball version, this game is highly competitive; therefore, groups should be formed with climbers of similar ability.

Variations

- Instead of acquiring letters as a penalty for failing to copy a sequence, students can acquire letters as a reward for copying the movements successfully. The winner is the first climber to spell the word *horse*.

- Decrease the challenge by using shorter words (such as *cat*), or increase the challenge by using longer words (*traversing*).

- Climbers can roll a die to determine the number of movements in a series.

- The first climber makes three movements, the next climber copies those movements and adds two more, the next climber copies those five and adds two more, and so on.

- Determine a point at which the climber must reverse direction.

Adapted, by permission, from J. Stiehl and T.B. Ramsey, 2005, *Climbing walls: A complete guide* (Champaign, IL: Human Kinetics), 118.

Mirroring

Overview

This activity is also known as Mirror Me. One climber is designated as the leader and directs or escorts a partner, small group, or entire class across the traverse wall.

Setup

No additional equipment is required.

Description

A designated leader begins to traverse a route of choice starting from one end of the traverse wall to the other. After the leader makes two or three climbing moves, subsequent climbers begin to mirror the leader by copying the same route. This activity promotes communication between climbers. Roles may change once the leader makes it across the wall or can no longer make a climbing move.

Variations

- To increase the challenge, leaders are required to make specific moves. For example, they might have to cross their feet or their hands once (instead of, say, leading with the same foot all the time, right leads and left crosses or steps ahead of the right foot), make two moves up before moving horizontally, or attempt an undercling or pinch grip at least once.

- Partners, teams, or the whole class can set a time limit for the traverse. Time the climbers, and have them switch roles at the end of the time.

- Add hoops of various sizes to the wall to increase the level of challenge. See the section titled Change the Components in chapter 1 (page 15) for ideas on placing hoops and other obstacles on the wall.

- Specify that only certain holds (such as blue or green) can be used.

- In teams of two, the leader and the follower can be connected with a short piece of string or yarn placed in their pockets. The team must work together to maintain a cooperative pace. To vary the challenge, make the yarn longer or shorter.

- Use string or yarn to connect a greater number of climbers and see how many students can traverse the wall without pulling the string from anyone's pocket (as shown in the photo).

Adapted, by permission, from J. Stiehl and T.B. Ramsey, 2005, *Climbing walls: A complete guide* (Champaign, IL: Human Kinetics), 109.

Limbo

Overview

Climbers attempt to traverse under a progressively lower limbo stick.

Setup

Attach limbo sticks (such as foam noodles or hoops) to the wall with tape or specially designed climbing holds, or nonclimbers can hold limbo sticks. Limbo music is optional.

Description

This activity is designed for pairs or small groups. Begin the game by attaching a limbo stick somewhere above the midpoint of the traverse wall. Climbers take turns attempting to traverse beneath a limbo stick. This activity is different from the traditional Limbo game in that students do not stand on the floor while moving under the limbo stick; they must be on the wall while climbing under the limbo stick. Each climber who successfully traverses below the limbo stick without touching it with any body part continues on to the next round. On subsequent rounds lower the limbo stick 12 inches (30 cm). The final climber able to traverse below the limbo stick without leaving the wall wins.

Variations

- Divide the wall into three to five sections; therefore, climbers can play three to five separate limbo games simultaneously. Overall winners from each of the sections can play one final game for the limbo championship.
- Instead of traversing below limbo sticks, students can play the game in reverse fashion: Climbers must traverse *over* the limbo stick. This variation would begin with the limbo stick at the bottom of the wall.
- Place hoops on the wall. Instead of going under, climbers must go through (as shown in the photo).
- Attach a series of hoops to the wall horizontally, increasing the limbo traverse distance on account of the extra movements needed to wind through the hoops.
- Attach a series of limbo sticks and hoops to the wall at various heights; climbers must decide whether to climb under, over, or through without touching any of them.

- As a follow-up to the previous variation, climbers follow one another on the wall. However, all followers must negotiate the obstacles in a different way than the leader did. For example, if the first climber goes under the first hoop and through the second, the next climber must go over or through the first hoop and over or below the second.

Order Out of Chaos

Overview

Collect pictures of items, which teammates must put in the correct order on an answer key. This activity works for many sequential items; the following example uses pictures of animals to create a food chain.

Setup

Next to handholds, tape pictures of various animals in the food chain (mosquito, chicken, cow, human). The pictures face the wall. You'll also need masking tape, a food chain answer key, and pens, pencils, or markers. (Show sample food chain answer key; include a list section and a chain section. You can find a sample food chain at www.sciencebob.com/lab/q-web-chain.html; click on the "Show Me Pictures!" link.)

Description

This small-group activity requires knowledge of the food chain. Taking turns, climbers retrieve a labeled animal card from the wall, bring it back to their group, and record the animal name in the list section on the group's answer key. The labeled animal card is then handed off to the next climber to return to any nonlabeled hold. After returning the labeled card, the climber must then retrieve another labeled card.

Every animal on the traverse wall must be represented on the answer key. The game ends when all groups have retrieved and recorded all of the animals from the food chain on their answer keys.

Variations

- The first team to complete their answer key wins; however, a penalty of 10 seconds is awarded for each animal out of place on the answer key. The teacher should time each group, and the winner is the group with the fastest overall time.
- Tape a shape on the wall to represent a food chain. Climbers then randomly pick labeled animal cards from a box and place them on the wall in an order representing the food chain.
- All climbers must come to a consensus on where any animal card from the food chain is placed on the wall.
- Increase the number of animal cards to change the level of challenge.
- As an off-wall activity, students can create cards of animals from the food chain.
- Instead of using animals in the food chain, arrange other items in their correct sequence. Here are examples:
  - Presidents of the United States: George Washington, John Adams, Thomas Jefferson, and so on
  - Wars with your country's involvement: for the United States, it could be American Revolution, Barbary Wars, War of 1812
  - Historical events
  - Numbers (for younger kids)
  - Book titles or authors (placed alphabetically)
  - Layers of the earth's surface (placed from outer to inner)
  - Steps for making a peanut butter and jelly sandwich
  - Stages of human development

Math and Numbers

Virtually any mathematical operation can be used in a traversing activity. You can expand the variety of activities in this chapter almost indefinitely. These activities also call for integrating math and climbing while encouraging collaboration between climbing instructors and classroom teachers. Climbing activities are closely associated with group members' ability to arrive at correct answers to mathematical problems. Many students enjoy these activities and often prefer tackling more difficult problems than solving easy (and thus less interesting) problems.

Math Matrix

Overview
Climbers locate numbers that, when entered in boxes in the top row and side row of a matrix, will create math problems to be solved by teammates.

Setup
Place numbers from 1 to 9 next to some holds. Have a matrix for each group. A sample matrix appears on the next page, but you can increase or decrease the size based on problem difficulty, the number of problems to solve, and the number of climbers in each group.

Description

When a climber reaches a numbered hold, she tells teammates that number. Teammates then enter the number in any empty square of their matrix, creating math problems as they fill the rows and columns. As each new problem appears, students solve the problem by multiplying the number in the shaded row by the number in the shaded column and recording the answer in the intersecting square.

For example, consider the sample matrix below. Let's say a climber finds the number 2 and his teammates record that number in the top row, between 4 and 7. Since the shaded column on the left side of the matrix already contains the numbers 6, 3, and 5, the students have created three new math problems.

- In the empty square where the 6 intersects with the 2, they record 12 (the product of 6 and 2).
- In the empty square where the 3 intersects with the 2, they record 6 (the product of 3 and 2).
- In the empty square where the 5 intersects with the 2, they record 10 (the product of 5 and 2).

Multiplication	4		7	6
6	24		42	
3	12		21	
5	20		35	

Variations

- Use other mathematical operations to either increase or decrease the difficulty of the problems: addition, subtraction, division.
- Increase the difficulty of numbers: two digits, fractions, decimals.
- Increase or decrease the size of the matrix (5 by 5, 5 by 7, 10 by 10).

- Provide the students with a matrix in which all the answers have been filled in. Teams must find numbers that will produce those answers and write the numbers in the shaded row and column. For example, if the number 24 is an answer in a multiplication matrix, students could locate 6 and 4, or 3 and 8.

Numbers Stretch

Overview

Climbers traverse the wall, stopping periodically to solve math problems.

Setup

Next to various handholds, place small cards with math problems written on one side and the solutions on the other side.

Description

This activity begins with a climber traversing the wall. When the spotter calls out, "Solution," the climber must provide an answer to the math problem that is written on the nearest card. Roles change when a climber provides an incorrect solution.

Variations

- Write multiplication table problems on one side of the card and the answer on the other. When the spotter calls out, "Product," the climber has 3 seconds to give an answer. Roles change when a climber gives no answer or an incorrect answer.
- Use simple division problems.
- Write unreduced fractions (such as 8/12) on one side of the card for students to reduce and some reduced fractions (for example, 1/3, 2/3, 1/2, 3/8) on the other. When the spotter calls out, "Reduce," the climber must choose the correctly reduced fraction (for example, 8/12 reduces to 2/3).
- Assign point values for math problems (for example, correct answer = 5 points; incorrect answer = –5 points). Climbers must attempt to solve a series of predetermined cards on the wall. The winner is the climber with the highest point value.

- A climber touches a number and then adds subsequent numbers to that number. Climb is complete when the total is 100.
- Place cards with math operators (such as +, −, =, ×, ÷) and numbers next to each handhold. Small groups create a route using the cards on the various handholds. The group provides another group a starting point, the number of operators used in the problem, and an end point. This group then attempts to re-create the route. For example, "Start at 7, use four math operators, and end with the answer 34." Here is a possible route:

  - Start at the number 7.
  - Move to a multiplication sign.
  - Move to the number 4.
  - Move to a division sign.
  - Move to the number 2.
  - Move to a multiplication sign.
  - Move to the number 3.
  - Move to a minus sign.
  - Move to the number 8.

- This route would create the following formula:
  $7 \times 4 \div 2 \times 3 - 8 = 34$

Familiar Products

Overview

Climbers locate numbers that become part of math problems (in this case, multiplication, hence "products").

Setup

Use beanbags, a number grid (made from painter's drop cloth or landscape fabric and colored tape; see the sample grid), and paper and pencils.

Description

A teammate approaches the grid and throws a beanbag onto it. The number on which the beanbag lands when multiplied (or added, subtracted, or divided) by the fifth number reached by the climber creates a problem for teammates to solve on a piece of paper. For example, one player's beanbag lands on 7. Meanwhile, after touching four numbers, the climber's fifth touch is 4. Teammates write "7 × 4 = 28" on their papers. If the beanbag lands on "free," teammates can enter any number they choose.

4	9	3	7	1
3	Free	7	5	2
1	8	2	9	4
7	6	Free	1	8
9	4	5	2	3

Variations

- Use other math operations (addition, subtraction, division).
- Each player tosses two beanbags. The *difference between* or the *product of* the two numbers is written on the paper.
- Change the numbers on the grid (such as two-digit, fractions, decimals), on the wall, or both.
- Players write the problems, but not the answers, and then exchange with another group to solve.

Math Stumper

Overview

Climbers locate numbers to solve math problems.

Setup

Place numbers next to various handholds. Write math problems on index cards.

Description

A climber must locate numbers that are the answers to various math problems. Teammates solve problems and direct the climber to the answers. For example, give the group the following problem. As they form the solution, group members direct the climber to locate the answers and "erase" them from consideration by touching them.

Problem: Erase 6 of 9 digits in the following numbers so that the results of the remaining numbers add up to 20.

Solution: In the top row, erase all three 7s. In the middle row, erase the first 1. In the bottom row, erase the first and second 9. That will leave 11 in the middle row and 9 in the bottom row, which add up to 20.

7	7	7
1	1	1
9	9	9

You can also increase the complexity of the math problem. For example: Erase 9 of 15 digits in the following box so that the remaining numbers add up to 1,111.

Solution: In the top row, erase the first and second 1. Erase all the 5s and 9s. This will leave 1 in the top row and 333 and 777 below, which add up to 1,111.

1	1	1
3	3	3
5	5	5
7	7	7
9	9	9

Variations

- Using a puzzle like *a* on the next page, arrange the digits 1, 2, 3, 4, and 5 in the circles so that the sum of three numbers in each direction is the same. Find as many combinations as you can. For each solution, the climber must locate the top three digits and then the bottom two digits, in that order. For example, to solve puzzle *a*, the climber must locate the digits in this order: 1, 3, 5, 2, and 4.

a

- Using a puzzle like *b* below, arrange the digits 2, 3, 4, 5, 6, 7, and 8 in the circles so that the sum of each straight line is 15.

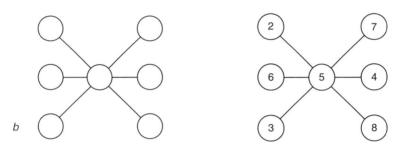

b

- Draw a bull's-eye diagram and place the numbers 31, 23, 11, and 5 in the circles as shown in *c* below. Pose this question to the team: "What numbers must an archer hit in order to score a total of 74 points?" As the team comes up with the solution (31, 11, 11, 11, 5, and 5), they direct the climber to find and touch the needed numbers. The climber can locate the numbers in any order, and the same number can be counted multiple times. Thus, in the example shown, the climber must find one 11 on the wall, not three different 11s.

- Increase the challenge of the bull's-eye variation by ruling that numbers on the wall count only once. Thus, in the example given, the climber must find three different 11s on the wall.

- Increase the challenge of the bull's-eye variation by ruling that the climber must touch the numbers in sequence from the center of the bulls'-eye outward.

- Increase the challenge of the bull's-eye variation by using six concentric circles instead of four. For example, fill in the circles with the numbers 40, 37, 24, 23, 17, and 16, and ask students to find a series that adds up to 100.

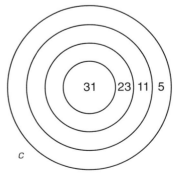

c

Bingo

Overview

Climbers traverse the wall, stopping periodically to touch numbered cards for off-wall students playing Bingo.

Setup

Next to various holds on the wall, place small cards with the numbers 0 to 40 written on them so the numbers are visible. You'll also need pencils and Bingo sheets (see page 77).

Description

This activity begins with two climbers traversing the wall. After making three climbing moves, a climber stops and calls out the number corresponding to the card next to his right hand. Numbers are called out in fairly rapid succession as students move across the wall. Students off the wall record these numbers on their Bingo sheets. When a student gets Bingo, she replaces a climber. After a number has been called out, the climber turns the card so that it faces the wall and can't be used until the next game.

Copy the sample Bingo sheet on page 77 for students. For variety, create additional sheets that have the numbers in different places.

Variations

- To increase the level of suspense, the game begins with the numbered Bingo cards facing the wall so that even the climbers don't know which numbers will be called next.
- Instead of numbers, the cards and sheets feature letters.
- Instead of numbers, the cards and sheets feature pictures of animals.
- If a climber gets tired, he switches places with a volunteer from off the wall.
- Climbers call out numbers after making more than three climbing moves.
- Climbers may choose to call out the number from the card next to the left or right hand or from the card near either foothold.
- A student off the wall chooses a series of five numbers, and the first person to get Bingo by using those numbers is the winner.

25	2	35	16	1
12	33	19	21	7
40	37	23	18	8
3	39	29	6	22
5	11	9	31	18

From J. Stiehl and D. Chase, 2008, *Traversing walls: 68 activities on and off the wall* (Champaign, IL: Human Kinetics).

- Increase or decrease the number of rows and columns on the Bingo sheets.
- Increase or decrease the range of numbers. For example, using the numbers from 0 to 100 will lengthen the activity and provide more climbing time.

High Roller

Overview

Climbers traverse the wall in search of the number that equals the sum of a pair of dice rolled.

Setup

You'll need several pairs of dice (large Styrofoam blocks work well, but dice also can be easily constructed from small square boxes). Next to various holds, place small pieces of masking tape with numbers written on them.

Description

One or two climbers begin this activity by traversing the wall. Another student rolls a pair of dice and calls out the two numbers rolled. The climbers must then traverse to a piece of masking tape that equals the sum of the dice. They can climb toward the same piece or to different pieces. The more pieces of tape on the wall, the faster the climbers will find the correct answer. New climbers begin after every three rolls.

Variations

- Climbers move only to odd- or even-numbered holds, attempting 10 total moves.
- Climbers continue to traverse until they reach a specified sum, such as 100.
- The wall can be divided into several sections according to degree of difficulty. For instance, in the more difficult section, fewer holds contain numbers. In the less difficult section, each hold has at least one number and many holds have several numbers.
- Climbers may choose to add or subtract the numbers of each roll. For example, if the student on the floor rolls 6 and 2, the climbers can try to find 8 (6 + 2) or 4 (6 − 2).

- Five students climb halfway up the wall, equally distant from one another. A student on the floor rolls dice to determine the climbers' movements. The first die indicates the number of movements, and the second die indicates the direction as follows:

  1 = up

  2 = down

  3 = right

  4 = left

  5 = back to previous hold

  6 = climber's choice

- Rolls of 3 and 4 mean the climbers make three moves to the left. Rolls of 1 and 2 mean the climbers make one move down. The object of the game is to remain on the wall for as long as possible. If a climber can't make the next move, a student from the floor takes his place. For safety reasons, climbers may not climb over or under one another.

- Instead of rolling small dice, construct large dice out of square boxes. On the sides of the first die, write these words: red, blue, orange, green, yellow, and black. On the sides of the second die, write these directions: up, down, left, right, back to start, and climber's choice. Using these dice, a roll of orange and left means the climber must move to an orange hold somewhere to his left.

Sudoku

Overview

After teammates solve a Sudoku problem, climbers traverse the wall in search of the numbers that were used to complete the problem.

Setup

You'll need numbers placed next to various holds. You'll also need Sudoku problems.

Description

In recent years, Sudoku has become a popular activity for children and adults. The puzzle is often published daily in the games section of newspapers. Sample puzzle a requires completing a grid so that each row, each column, and each 2 × 3 box contains every digit from 1 to 6, with no repeats. The numbers in white boxes are provided for climbers; the numbers in shaded boxes are filled in by the climbers.

Variations

- Use a simpler Sudoku puzzle, but require the climber to locate every number. In sample puzzle b, the climber must touch four 1s, four 2s, and so on. Alternatively, the climber could touch the numbers in sequence (1 then 2 then 3 then 4, and then start over with a different 1, a different 2, and so on).
- Change the grid configuration and apply different rules. To solve sample puzzle c, students must arrange the numbers from 1 to 9 in the bubbles so that each side of the triangle adds up to the same total.

3	6	4	1	2	5
1	2	5	3	6	4
5	3	6	4	1	2
4	1	2	5	3	6
6	4	1	2	5	3
2	5	3	6	4	1

a

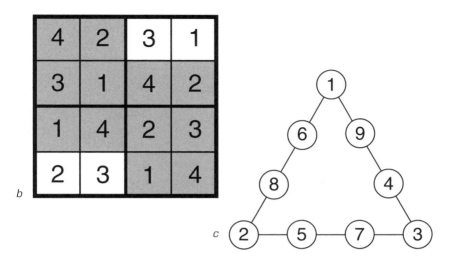

b

c

Magic Square

Overview

Climbers traverse the wall in search of numbers in sequence.

Setup

Randomly place numbers next to various holds. You'll also need Magic Square math problems.

Description

A magic square is an arrangement of numbers from 1 to n^2 (such as 1 to 4, 1 to 9, 1 to 16) placed in a matrix. Each number occurs only once, and the sum of the entries in any row, column, or main diagonal is the same. Sample a shows a 3 × 3 magic square.

To begin this activity, teammates complete a magic square, and the climber locates and touches in sequence the numbers used in the square. The group receives points for solving the square and for touching all numbers in sequence.

Variations

- To decrease the challenge, require that only sums for rows or only sums for columns must be the same.

- To increase the challenge, ask the climber to locate any 12 numbers on the wall. Teammates then select 9 of the 12 numbers to complete the magic square.
- To make the activity considerably more challenging, have the group use the numbers 1 to 16 to create a 4 × 4 magic square instead. Sample *b* shows one possible solution.
- Instead of having one student climb to all numbers, teammates take turns on the wall until the group finds all numbers required to solve the puzzle.
- Change the grid configuration and apply different rules. To solve sample puzzle *c*, students must arrange the numbers 1 to 8 in the bubbles so that each number's neighbor is at least 2 higher than it or 2 lower than it. For example, students can't put 2 or 4 in any bubble that touches a bubble containing the number 3.

8	1	6
3	5	7
4	9	2

a

1	15	14	4
12	6	7	9
8	10	11	5
13	3	2	16

b

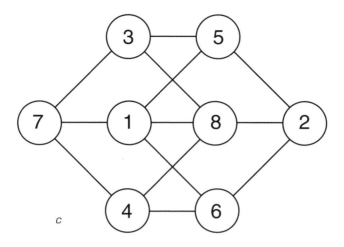

c

- Change the grid configuration to a star and apply different rules. To solve sample puzzle *d*, students must arrange the numbers 16, 18, 20, 22, 24, 26, 28, 28, 32, 36 in the bubbles so that each row of four bubbles adds up to 100.

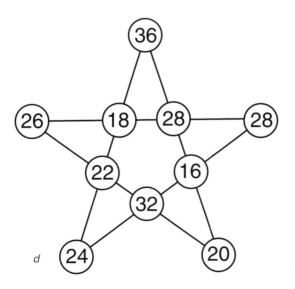

d

- Change the grid configuration to connected hexagons and apply different rules. To solve sample puzzle *e*, students must arrange the numbers 1 to 9 in the bubbles so the numbers around each hexagon add up to 30. Students can use the numbers more than once, and not every number will be used.

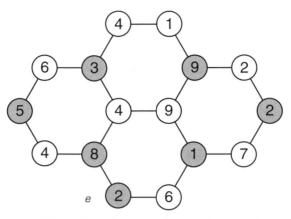

- Use letter problems. To solve sample puzzle *f*, students must replace the letters with any numbers from 1 to 9 to create a math problem that is correct as shown. Solution: A is 2, B is 1, C is 7, and D is 8.

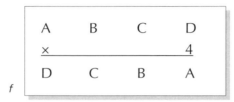

- Ask teams to determine the next number in a sequence. For example, in sample puzzle *g*, the next number would be 28. (Add 2 to the first number to get the second number, add 3 to the second number to get the third number, add 4 to the third number to get the fourth number, and so on.)

- Ask teams to complete an entirely blank puzzle. To solve sample puzzle *h*, students must fill the blank slots in the puzzle with the numbers from 1 to 6, using each number only once.

Words and Letters

Fun-filled climbing activities can facilitate learning of important academic skills, which all too often have been drilled into some children's psyches in unpleasant ways. The cognitive challenges involved both in climbing and in using and understanding written language can make learning more palatable and effective. Whether it involves early efforts at letter recognition or advanced comprehension of complex reading tasks, climbing in connection with word use can benefit many youngsters and adults. Whereas the previous chapter focused on mathematical operations, this chapter focuses on reading and writing, specifically words and letters.

The Case of the Missing Vowels

Overview

Climbers locate vowels that are missing from familiar phrases. For example, making sense of the Shakespeare quote "T b, r nt t b" ("To be, or not to be") would require inserting several missing vowels.

Setup

Place vowels next to various handholds. You'll also need a sentence, paragraph, or passage from which vowels have been removed.

Description

A climber must locate vowels that have been removed from a written statement. As the climber reaches a new vowel, teammates complete the missing work. For example, "Y cn rd wtht vwls f y wrk hrd. Smtms t's sy, bt smtms t's hrd!" (Answer: You can read without vowels if you work hard. Sometimes it's easy, but sometimes it's hard!)

Try using words with a common theme. For example, each of the following math-related words is missing its vowels:

- lgbr (algebra)
- vrbl (variable)
- sbtrctn (subtraction)
- fctr (factor)
- prdct (product)
- lgrthm (algorithm)

- cmpst (composite)
- dcml (decimal)
- qtnt (quotient)
- ngl (angle)
- ght (eight)

Variations

- Vowels must be located in the order in which they are missing.
- Remove some consonants instead of vowels, or remove some of both. (Remember to place the missing consonants next to holds on the wall.)
- Changing one letter at a time, make at least six different words. Try starting with simple words such as *try, sack, rock,* or *gold.* For example, you can change *bean* to *loud* like this:

BEAN → BEAR → BOAR → ROAR → ROAD → LOAD → LOUD

- Give players a sentence that they must complete. For example, in the first tongue twister listed below, the missing word is "father." Remove words from the other examples to create challenges for students, and have them practice saying the completed tongue twisters several times.

  – Francis Fletcher fried fifty flounders for Fatty Fifer's _ _ _ _ _ _.
  – Old oily Ollie oils old oily autos.
  – Six slippery sliding snakes slither swiftly.
  – The clothes moth's mouth closed.

What Do You Mean?

Overview

Climbers traverse the wall, stopping periodically to define a given word.

Setup

Next to various handholds, place small cards with a vocabulary word written on one side and the definition on the other.

Description

This activity begins with a climber traversing the wall. When the spotter or a designated non-climber calls out, "Define," the climber must define the vocabulary word that is written on the nearest card. The spotter or non-climber can choose when to call out for a definition, or the call could be based on the roll of a die (e.g., odd number; 1 or 6) or some other method. Roles change when a climber defines a word incorrectly.

Variations

- Before looking at the definition, the climber and spotter must come to an agreement on the definition. If an agreement cannot be made, the spotter or climber may challenge one another. The winner of the challenge becomes the climber. If there is no winner, roles remain the same.
- Place cards on the wall with the definition facing out. When the spotter calls out, "Word," the climber must give the word that corresponds to the definition.
- Instead of using vocabulary words, write various cultural celebrations (such as Christmas, Chanukah, Kwanzaa) on the cards. When the spotter calls out, "Define," the climber must provide information that describes that celebration.
- Assign point values for definitions (for example, correct answer = 5 points, incorrect answer = –5 points). Climbers must attempt to define a series of predetermined cards on the wall. The winner is the climber with the highest point value.
- Roles change at a set time.

Word Circle

Overview

Climbers locate letters, which teammates use to create words.

Setup

Place letters next to various holds. You'll also need a Word Circle sheet.

Description

Each team has a Word Circle sheet that features eight letters—the first letters in words that must be completed. The climber locates vowels on the wall and calls them out to her teammates, who write each new vowel in the shaded ring of the Word Circle. Each time they add a vowel, the teammates can begin suggesting words that begin with the two letters shown.

For example, the Word Circle below includes the initial letter V. If the climber finds and calls out an A, his teammates can write that vowel in the shaded section next to the V and then write down any words they can think of that begin with VA (such as *van, vacuum,* or *valedictorian*).

As an added twist, the center of the Word Circle specifies the type of word that is allowed. In the example below, all words must be nouns, so students can't contribute words such as *vanish* or *vain*.

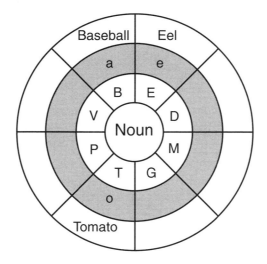

Variations

- Limit the number of letters in each answer (such as at least 6 letters or no more than 6 letters).
- Develop as many words as possible for each answer. The sample Word Circle includes *baseball,* but players could also come up with *bat, battleship, ballroom,* and so on.
- Teammates can suggest words only while their climber is on the wall.
- Change the part of speech given in the center of the Word Circle. Instead of nouns, students could try to come up with verbs, adjectives, or adverbs.
- Instead of providing only the first letter, the Word Circle could provide the first two letters of each word, such as TA or FR.
- Require that all words *end with* the letters provided. For example, if students wrote the letter A in the shaded section next to the letter V, they could suggest words such as *java, nova,* and *lava.*
- On the wall, specify whether a letter is a long vowel or a short vowel, and require that teammates stick to that distinction when coming up with words. In the sample Word Circle, if A is specified as a long vowel, teammates could suggest *vagrant* but not *vampire.*
- Teams later incorporate their words into a story, poem, or song.

Jumble

Overview

Climbers locate cards with jumbled words, which teammates must rearrange.

Setup

Place cards with jumbled words next to holds, blank side out; some cards are blank on both sides.

Description

The climber moves along the wall looking for cards that have jumbled words on the reverse side. After locating a jumbled word, the climber calls out the letters to her teammates, who write them down and try to unscramble them. For example, *risecu* becomes *cruise*; *folggin* becomes *golfing*; *crnasa* becomes *NASCAR*; and, *selbbaal* becomes *baseball*.

Create word jumbles of varying difficulty, suitable for various age groups, and provide clues if desired. The following is a sample list of easier words and clues; the next list offers slightly more challenging jumbles.

Easier Jumbles

BELOW: part of a person (elbow)

RITE: something on a car (tire)

RING: a big smile (grin)

CARE: a competitive run (race)

STEM: name of a baseball team (Mets)

DOOM: your temperament (mood)

LOOTS: a wooden chair (stool)

DAWN: a magic stick (wand)

SKIN: something to wash your hands in (sink)

PAWS: an insect (wasp)

WORTH: done with a ball (throw)

HOSES: placed on your feet (shoes)

RESIST: opposite of brother (sister)

BRUSH: a plant (shrub)

More Challenging Jumbles

LIVED: a bad creature (devil)

NAILS: slow mover (snail)

LUMBER: a fight (rumble)

WENT: an amphibian (newt)

BURY: a jewel (ruby)

DROP: move people along (prod)

GRIP: an uptight, stuffy person (prig)

Variations

- Award additional points if a scrambled word can be rearranged into more than one word. For example, *saerc* could become *scare*, *acres*, or *races*. You can give the students hints by working all the possible words into a sentence. Here's an example:
  - My little brother hit his head on a door_____ and it went _____. (*knob, bonk*)
  - I walked almost one _____ to find a _____ tree. (*mile, lime*)
  - I got pricked by a _____ and it made my thumb _____. (*rose, sore*)
  - We saw a hairy brown _____ stuck in the hot _____. (*rat, tar*)
  - Yesterday she _____ some bread and drank some _____. (*ate, tea*)

- Climbers call out the jumbled letters for other teams to unscramble. The team that solves their jumbles in the least amount of time is the winner.

- To increase the challenge, incorporate a bonus puzzle. Set up the wall with several colored cards, and have the climbers turn over only cards of that color. The back of each card contains a jumble that includes one or more underlined letters. The climber's teammates unscramble the words on a worksheet, on which the letters needed for the bonus puzzle have already been underlined. Here's an example:

Cards on wall	Solutions on worksheet
L I V A L	V I L L A
S Y S A G	G A S S Y
H I P L A C	C A L I P H
B I M E B I	I M B I B E

After the students unscramble each word, they use only the under lined letters to form the bonus answer. Provide them with a hint, such as the following:

"What did the generous police officer do when he stopped the quarterback for speeding?"

HE _ _ _ _   _ _ _   A   " _ _ _ _ ."

Underlined letters: V A G S S A P H I M E

Answer: HE GAVE HIM A "PASS."

- Use word riddles instead of jumbles. Word riddles disguise common words, phrases, places, and sayings. For example, the word riddles below communicate the following phrases: *(a) good afternoon, (b) read between the lines,* and *(c) jack in the box.*

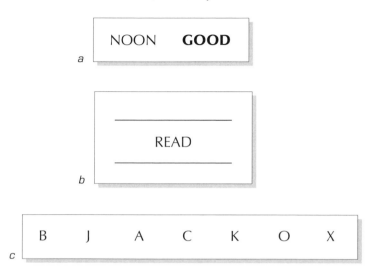

- Use word shuffles instead of jumbles. A climber selects seven letters from cards placed near holds. Each card features a letter and a designated number of points. The climber's teammates use as many of the seven letters as they can to form a word and determine the total point value. For example, say the climber selects the following seven letters (point values given in parentheses):

T (2),　R (2),　O (2),　E (1),　P (6),　R (2),　S (2)

Forming the word *stop* would be worth 12 points, and forming the word *porters* would be worth 17 points. Applying a rule of 30 bonus points for using all letters would result in a 47-point word.

- Students on the floor must solve a puzzle by separating a group of letters into two shorter words. When certain letters are removed in order, those letters form one word, and the remaining letters form the second word. Once the students find the solution, they direct the climber to locate and touch each letter to be removed, in order. Following are samples and hints:

Puzzle: hucmaarn
Hint: Remove the people and leave the van.
Answers: human, car

Puzzle: stbaurrst
Hint: Remove the sun and leave the explosion.
Answers: star, burst

Puzzle: wpanolthfer
Hint: Remove the cat and leave the dog.
Answers: panther, wolf

Puzzle: mapacloren
Hint: Remove the tree and leave the nut.
Answers: maple, acorn

Puzzle: miminnickeey
Hint: Remove the girl mouse and leave the boy mouse.
Answers: Minnie, Mickey

Puzzle: swpiedebr
Hint: Remove the bug and leave its home.
Answers: spider, web

Puzzle: cmoffugee
Hint: Remove the drink and leave the cup.
Answers: coffee, mug

Puzzle: edsutcuatdorent
Hint: Remove the teacher and leave the kid.
Answers: educator, student

Puzzle: rfabobitx
Hint: Remove the prey and leave the predator.
Answers: rabbit, fox

Funny Fill-In

Overview

Participants are provided a story—the more humorous the better—from which certain key words are missing. Climbers locate cards on the wall that specify the type of word needed to fill in each blank, and their teammates find appropriate words to complete the story.

Setup

Near holds on the wall, place small cards that feature various types of words, such as nouns, verbs, adjectives, adverbs, numbers, and names of colors. Create a box of word cards that offer specific examples of those types of words.

Description

Write a brief, simple story and omit some key words, such as nouns, adjectives, and verbs, which must be inserted to complete the story. (See page 95 for a sample.) An easy way to do this is to choose a paragraph from any publication and leave out every fifth main word.

The climber locates various word types on the wall and calls them out to a searcher on the floor. Next, the searcher chooses appropriate words from the box of word cards and hands them to a teammate, who writes the words in the correct blank spaces in the story. The writer doesn't tell anyone what the story is about.

Climbers and searchers can exchange roles as the story develops, but the writer must continue until all the words have been filled in. The writer then reads the completed story out loud. Depending on the cards that the searcher chose from the box, the story might be funny, ridiculous, or just plain strange.

Sample Word Cards

- **Nouns:** nose, coach, bicycle, cat, umbrella, goldfish, sidewalk
- **Verbs:** run, swim, yawn, pitch, sneeze, crush, tickle, confuse
- **Adjectives:** friendly, itchy, brave, excessive, messy, plump, smelly, broken, pitiful
- **Adverbs:** carefully, stupidly, greedily, happily, outside
- **Numbers:** 4, 11, 70
- **Colors:** violet, orange, silver

Training for Climbing

For years, people thought climbing was an activity for athletes who

were strong, _____, and _____. But today,
               adjective   *adjective*

every Tom, Dick, and _____ can do it
                     silly first name

because of new _____ training methods.
              adjective

Climbers have to give up _____ and most _____.
                verb ending in "-ing"   *verb ending in "-ing"*

They eat lots of _____ and fresh _____ vegetables.
          a food   *a color*

Every morning, they spend _____ hours stretching their
                    a number

_____ and touching their _____. Then they spend
plural body part   *plural body part*

two hours lifting _____ and _____ until
              plural noun   *verb ending in "-ing"*

their pulse gets up to _____.
                 a number

Afterward, they traverse the wall _____ times, and on their
                     a number

final traverse, they use only their fingers and their _____.
                                        plural body part

All this exercise strengthens their _____ so they'll be
                       plural noun

ready to compete in other activities, such as _____ or
                            verb ending in "-ing"

even _____. You can always tell a serious climber by the
  verb ending in "-ing"

_____ expression on his or her _____.
  adjective   *noun*

From J. Stiehl and D. Chase, 2008, *Traversing walls: 68 activities on and off the wall* (Champaign, IL: Human Kinetics).

Variations

- Use even more kinds of words, such as animals, body parts, geographical locations (such as Spain, Cleveland, or the bathroom), or exclamations or silly words (such as *wow, ouch,* or *whomp*).
- Students create the stories and word cards themselves and then trade them with other teams. The stories can be on any topic deemed appropriate for the class.
- Students need not limit themselves to stories but could also create poems, letters, songs, recipes, interviews, and so on, as long as they omit some of the key words.
- If students are stumped for ideas, they can modify familiar songs or poems to remove the key words. For example, the song "Oh, Susanna" works well for younger kids.

Anagram

Overview

Climbers search for letters underneath pieces of paper or cardboard to spell an anagram.

Setup

You'll need masking tape and small cards (some blank and others with letters written on them). All are taped next to holds. Conceal the letters by facing the letters to the wall surface.

Description

Climbers traverse the wall searching for letters concealed behind cards. The climber should find a predetermined number of letters. As each letter is found, the climbers call them out to their partners on the floor, who must spell one or more anagrams using the pool of letters. For example, included in the nine letters the climber finds are E, I, V, and L, and his partner rearranges these letters to spell *live* and *evil* (or *veil* and *vile*). After a partner spells an anagram, partners switch roles.

Variations

- Partners switch roles after locating one letter.
- Instead of using anagrams, rearrange letters to form words to fill in the blanks in various sentences. For example, a climber might locate the

letters N, U, F, Y, and N, and his partner uses them to complete the sentence, "The class looked _____ on the traverse wall" *(funny)*.

- Use cards of varied colors to distinguish vowels from consonants. For example, hide vowels behind the blue cards and consonants behind the yellow cards.

- Each partner has a specified amount of time to traverse the wall and collect as many letters as possible. After both partners have had a turn, they spell as many different words as they can from their pool of letters.

- Instead of rearranging letters to spell words, the students must find whole words and use them to create a full sentence.

Spell It

Overview

Climbers traverse the wall touching the holds representing the letters in a given word.

Setup

Underneath the climbing holds, place small pieces of tape with letters of the alphabet. Words that can be created using those letters are written on pieces of paper and placed in a box.

Description

Spell It can be played in pairs or in small groups. Each student takes a turn choosing a word from the box and traversing the wall, touching holds that correspond to the letters in that word. The climber must touch all letters in the word, but he can touch them in any sequence.

Variations

- To make the activity easier, place multiple letters at each hold. Climbers can select any of the letters available.
- To make the activity harder, climbers must touch letters in sequence.
- Instead of spelling a word drawn from the box, climbers can spell their names.
- If a letter appears more than once in a word, such as the R in *mirror,* climbers have to touch that letter only once.
- If a letter appears more than once in a word, climbers must touch each letter on the wall separately. For example, to spell *mirror,* a climber would have to touch three different holds that feature the letter R.
- Rather than touch each letter in a word, climbers choose full sentences from the box and traverse the wall to touch each word.
- Climbers accumulate letters as they traverse, trying not to spell a word. The game begins with three letters already established, such as FAI. The first climber traverses until he finds a letter to add that will not spell a word; he might choose P, but he can't choose R (which would spell *fair*) or L (which would spell *fail*). The next climber then tries to add another letter without spelling a word. When a climber is forced to spell a word, he earns one of the letters in the word *ghost,* and anyone who receives all five letters is eliminated. The winner is the last climber to spell *ghost.*
- Instead of using letters or words, climbers choose a number from the box and must traverse the wall, touching numbered holds to reach the sum. You can increase the challenge by placing higher numbers farther away on the wall, which increases the climbing time.
- Do the previous variation, but climbers must subtract each touched number from the chosen number until they reach 0.
- Climbers traverse the wall in the sequence of their telephone numbers; using area codes increases the traverse time.

Adapted, by permission, from J. Stiehl and T.B. Ramsey, 2005, *Climbing walls: A complete guide* (Champaign, IL: Human Kinetics), 110-111.

Text Messaging

Overview

Teammates answer questions and the climber locates corresponding letter answers.

Setup

Place a letter of the alphabet next to a hold. You'll need a list of questions to be answered by using one or two letters from the alphabet.

Description

Teammates are given definitions and must come up with answers that can be expressed using one or two letters of the alphabet. Climbers then locate the holds marked with the matching letters. Following are sample definitions and answers:

An insect that stings (B)

A large body of water (C)

A question asked (Y)

A female sheep (U)

A green vegetable (P)

A blue bird (J)

A drink (T)

Myself (I)

Opposite of full (MT)

Number after 79 (AT)

A crawling plant (IV)

Having many seeds (CD)

A type of tent (TP)

Rot away (DK)

Pretty person (QT)

Girl's name (KT, KC, or LN)

Boy's name (ON or PT)

All right (OK)

Jealousy (NV)

Not difficult (EZ)

A written composition (SA)

Variations

- Groups compete for time to complete all questions. Each climber locates one answer, either in sequence or in no prescribed order.

- Teams earn bonus points for creating additional puzzles, especially if they can baffle other groups.

- Play License Plate, where climbers must locate all the letters needed to spell out an abbreviation. For example, BA2NA is an abbreviation for *banana,* requiring the climber to locate B, A, N, A, N, A (in sequence or in any order).

- Create (or challenge teams to create) longer puzzles. For example, "How a baby might say the name of a chocolate cookie" (OEO).

Telegram

Overview

Climbers locate letters, and teammates must use them as beginning letters of words in a telegram.

Setup

Place letters of the alphabet next to various holds.

Description

A climber locates a specified number of letters and calls them out to teammates, who write them down in any order. Each member of the team then composes a telegram that uses each letter as the first letter in a word of the message. The messages can be strange, but they must make sense. For example, the letters C, I, A, T, I, and S could become any of the following messages:

- Climbing is awesome. Try it sometime.
- Can insects attack tents? I'm scared!
- Can Isabelle alter Tom's initial statement?
- Careful investigators assess the Iditarod statistics.

After each teammate has composed at least one message, other players read them aloud to the whole group.

Variations

- To make the activity easier, students are allowed to add extra words to the message. For example, a telegram using C, I, A, T, I, and S might read as follows:
    - Come in and watch television in style.
    - Can I find a turtle in the swamp?
- An even simpler version allows students to arrange the selected letters in any order. Thus, if a climber finds C, I, A, T, I, and S, a telegram might read this way:
    - Alas, I think it showed courage!
    - I sat in the apple crisp.
    - Try catching a snake in Italy.
    - Some thief ate Ian's ice cream!

- To increase the challenge, at least two letters (of the climber's choice) must be used more than once. Using the previous example, the climber might require that his teammates use the letter T twice and the letter C three times. Thus, they must compose a telegram out of words beginning with C, C, C, I, A, T, T, I, and S.
- Teammates hand a completed telegram to another team. During the next round, that team must reply to the telegram using the new set of letters found by their climber.
- Climbers call out letters for another team, trying to choose letters that will make it hard for them to write a telegram.

Code Breaker

Overview

Climbers locate coded letters that correspond to letters that teammates use to decipher a message.

Setup

Place 26 coded letters next to some holds (for example, A = ☼, B = ♀, C = ☺, D = ♥). You'll also have a message to be deciphered, such as this:

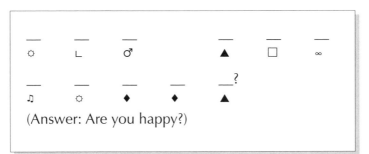

(Answer: Are you happy?)

Description

Climbers traverse the wall, looking for coded letters. They call out each new code to their teammates, who must use the codes to decipher a secret message. Climbers and teammates can exchange roles at any time.

Variations

- Teams send secret messages to other teams, and students must reply in code.
- Use different codes, such as Morse code, Braille, or a code that substitutes numbers for letters.

Scattered Categories

Overview

Climbers locate letters that are then used by teams to create words in various categories.

Setup

You'll need two decks of cards (one with letters of the alphabet, the other with categories). Place alphabet cards facedown next to holds; place category cards facedown on the floor.

Description

When a climber finds a letter near a hold, he calls it out to the whole class. Flip over a category card and announce the category to the class. Then each team tries to come up with a word that fits the category and that starts with the required letter. For example, if the climber calls out, "O," and the category is birds, one answer would be owl.

The first team to find a word wins the card for that category. The object of the game is to collect the most category cards.

Examples of categories:

State	Country	President
Make of car	Cereal brand	Color
Nonsense word	Book title	Magazine title
Type of dog	Vegetable	Type of sandwich
Cartoon character	Movie star	TV show
Candy bar	Author	Man's name
U.S. city	Sport	Famous singer
Something green	Fruit	Inventors
Explorers	Cartoon characters	Comic strip characters
Famous couples	Stadiums	Sports team names
State capitals	Foreign capitals	Types of vehicles
Ice cream flavors	Popular song titles	National/state holidays
Famous Americans	Book titles	

Variations

- The winning team is the one that collects a specified number of category cards.

- To increase the difficulty, the climber calls out two letters, and teams must come up with two answers for the category, one beginning with each letter.
- To decrease the difficulty, the climber calls out multiple letters. Teams come up with only one answer, but their answer can start with any of the called letters. For example, if the climber finds M, W, and T, and the category is U.S. states, teams could name any state that begins with M, W, or T.
- Instead of coming up with a word that begins with the chosen letter, teams must find a word that *ends* with that letter.
- Teams must come up with a word in which the chosen letter appears twice. For example, if the climber calls out N and the category is fruit, teams couldn't give *orange* as an answer (which has only one N) but could answer *banana* (which has two Ns).

Caught Off Guard

Overview

While traversing, climbers call out categories for which teammates must create words in that category.

Setup

On the floor, stack cards with a list of categories (see page 102 for sample categories).

Description

Before getting on the wall, a climber selects a category card from the stack on the floor. The card lists three categories—for example, shoes, flowers, and birds. The climber announces the categories to her team and begins traversing the wall. At any point, the climber calls out a category and the name of a teammate (such as "Shoes, Erin!") and that person must answer within 3 seconds (Erin must name a kind of shoe). If the teammate is caught off guard and fails to respond or gives an incorrect answer, the climber is awarded a point.

The climber tries to acquire as many points as possible before she tires of traversing or completes a certain route. A good strategy to catch a teammate off guard is to call on that person several times in a row, using the same category each time.

Variations

- Instead of answering within 3 seconds, the teammate must answer before the climber reaches two more holds.
- The climber calls out a letter and, within a set time limit, his teammates must name any six objects that begin with that letter. For example, if the climber calls "G," teammates could answer *goggles, glass, glove, glue, grass,* and *guitar.*
- Roles are reversed: Teammates try to stump the climber. If a climber is stumped, a teammate can take his place on the wall.

Just the Facts

Overview

Gathering information from two climbers, teammates fill in as many blanks on their scorecards as possible.

Setup

Next to holds, place cards with categories (such as movie titles, singers, living creatures). Also place letters of the alphabet next to holds. You'll need scorecards as well.

Description

This activity is similar to other category games but involves two climbers on the wall at the same time. The first climber traverses to a card next to a hold and announces the category written on that card. The second climber traverses to a different card and announces the letter written on it. Each team on the floor must name an item that fits the category and begins with the letter.

For example, the first climber calls out "Vegetables," and the second climber calls out the letter B. One team might answer "Brussels sprouts," while another answers "Broccoli."

Climbers continue finding cards, switching back and forth between categories and letters each time. The game ends after a specified time or after either climber finishes traversing a set route.

You can expand this activity by having each student on the floor fill out a scorecard that has 25 blanks (five rows of letters and five columns of categories). First, a climber locates five category cards on the wall that seem appealing. She can announce the categories one at a time, or she can wait and announce them after collecting all five cards. Next, the second climber locates five letter cards on the wall, and again can announce them one at a time or at the end. As the categories and letters are announced, the students on the floor fill in their scorecards with the five categories across the top and the five letters down the left side.

At that point, teams fill in the 25 blanks with answers (see the sample scorecard). Each answer must fit the given category and start with the given letter. When time is up, teams exchange scorecards to see which team earned the most points.

Scorecard

Team ___Brainiacs___

Category	Baseball player	World leader	Brass instrument	Jewelry item	Vegetable
T	Joe Torres		Tuba	Tiara	Turnip
M	Mickey Mantle			Money clip	
C		Winston Churchill		Charm bracelet	Carrot
Wild	Hank Aaron		French horn	Earrings	Onion
R	Babe Ruth	Ronald Reagan		Ring	Radish

Variations

- Students can use a specific answer only once on the scorecard even though it might be a valid answer for a different category or letter.

- A few letter cards on the wall are wild cards, which means that students can write any letter in that spot on their scorecard.

- The game uses only one climber, who selects five category cards but only one letter card. Students write the same letter for all five rows of their scorecard. Thus, for each category, they must come up with five different answers that begin with the same letter. (You can exclude wild cards and difficult letters such as Q and X from the wall.)

- To increase the degree of difficulty, add subcategories. For example, a card that says "book" might also name a specific kind of book, such as fiction, nonfiction, children's, mystery, romance, science fiction, and so on. The category "famous world leaders" might specify living, dead, male, female, politician, educator, and so on.

6

Adventure Travel

This chapter focuses on activities that involve simulated traveling to various destinations, such as U.S. states, countries, the summit of Mount Everest, and even the moon. Other travel activities include time elements or combine group activities on and off the wall. Many activities in this chapter also require the creative use of props. Some need only a few items—in Bell Ringer, for example, you simply attach several bells to the traverse wall—while others require more elaborate setup, such as the activity stations for Wall Obstacle Course. For some activities, travel from point to point requires considerable planning and cooperation, whereas for other activities, the major challenge is largely physical.

Olympic Traverse

Overview

Climbers touch a predetermined number of holds in a specified sequence or a set amount of time. Points are collected over time in order to attain various levels of achievement.

Setup

Differentiate the holds by color, size, shape, or another method. You'll need ribbons, certificates, wall charts, or other small awards to acknowledge completion of various levels of challenge.

Description

This activity allows for progressive improvement. For instance, to achieve Olympic training status, a climber might need to touch 10 holds in 40 seconds. Doing this 10 times earns a bronze medal, doing it 15 times earns a silver medal, and doing it 20 times earns a gold medal. To achieve Olympic qualifying status, a climber might need to touch 15 holds in 50 seconds, and to achieve Olympic games status, a climber might need to touch 25 holds in 1 minute. Feel free to adjust the task (the number of holds or completions required) to fit the abilities of the climbers.

Sample Chart for Olympic Traverse

	Bronze	Silver	Gold
Olympic training status 10 holds in 40 seconds	10 completions	15 completions	20 completions
Olympic qualifying status 15 holds in 50 seconds	10 completions	20 completions	25 completions
Olympic games status 25 holds in 1 minute	10 completions	25 completions	30 completions

Variations

- Find students in another school that follows a similar traversing program and ask them to be pen pals (or e-mail pals) with the students in your class. Pen pals could write to each other about their experiences on the wall, or they could focus on specific themes (such as physiology, stamina, or the factors that influence balance) or styles of writing (such as haiku).

- Allow students to earn points in a variety of categories over an extended time. For example, in each class session, students might select a category from the following list and then gain points based on their achievements in that category. Encourage achievements in personal conditioning and supporting others as well as in climbing. Physical ability is important, but alternative avenues for success can motivate less-skilled climbers.

  - Appropriate warm-ups (1 warm-up = 3 points, 2 warm-ups = 6 points, 3 warm-ups = 10 points)
  - Difficult moves (2 moves = 5 points, 4 moves = 10 points, 6 moves = 15 points; although the climber isn't being tested, the difficulty of moves will need to be determined by the instructor based on knowledge of climbers' abilities)
  - Time on the wall (up to 3 minutes = 5 points; more than 3 minutes = 10 points; at least 4 minutes = 15 points)
  - Spotting (3 points for each climber spotted, up to 15 points)
  - Balance stations (off-wall activity; specified points for each station, or for accomplishments at each station)
  - Flexibility and strength exercises (off-wall activity, similar to warm-ups)

Bell Ringer

Overview

Climbers traverse the wall from opposite ends, ringing a bell that is attached to the wall.

Setup

Divide the wall into two halves with two to seven bells attached at various heights at the midpoint of the wall.

Description

This activity is designed for two small-sided teams. One team begins on the left side of the wall and the other begins on the right. At your signal, the first climber from each team traverses to the midpoint of the wall and rings a bell. The first two climbers step off the wall, and the next two begin their traverse toward the bells. The first team to cycle all of its climbers through the activity wins.

Variations

- Each climber on the team must ring the bell with a different body part, such as the hand, foot, chin, or elbow.
- Attach the bells at the left and right sides of the wall instead of the midpoint. Each climber traverses to the midpoint and back before ringing the bell.
- Encourage strategy by limiting the number of climbers allowed to ring any given bell. For example, if you have 10 climbers and five bells, make a rule that only two people can ring each bell and then it becomes off limits.
- Replace bells with beanbags, bandannas, or tennis balls. The first climber retrieves one of the objects and traverses back to the starting point. The next climber replaces that object before continuing the process.
- Opposing teams can set specific routes, and climbers can follow only those routes during the original game.
- The entire class can compete against the clock, trying for a record time.

Adapted, by permission, from J. Stiehl and T.B. Ramsey, 2005, *Climbing walls: A complete guide* (Champaign, IL: Human Kinetics), 117.

Traverse for Time

Overview

Climbers chart their cumulative time on the traverse wall.

Setup

You'll need individual time cards (include climber's name, date, and time on wall), a clock, and pencils.

Description

This activity lets climbers assess their personal improvement by charting their progress in "climb time," meaning the overall time spent climbing (not counting resting on the wall or performing off-wall activities). Feel free to use the sample progress card on page 112 or develop your own. Climbers try to increase their individual climb time in each class session, thereby increasing their cardiorespiratory and muscular endurance. For example, if a student climbed for 11 minutes during Monday's class, she'd try to climb for at least 12 minutes in the next class.

Variations

- After determining their climb time for one class session, students predict their total climb time for the next 10 sessions. For added challenge, students could try to increase their climb time by a set amount in each session. For example, if a student climbs for 4 minutes during the first class and wants to increase her climb time by 10% in each subsequent class, she needs to climb for 4 minutes, 24 seconds in the next session.

- Climbers can chart the number of times they complete a horizontal lap (traversing from the far left of the wall to the far right and back) or a vertical lap (traversing from the far bottom of the wall to the top and back).

- Climbers set time goals—for example, planning to climb for 3 minutes—and stop after reaching the goal, or choose to push past it.

- Climbers follow a series of predetermined routes.

- Climbers try to beat their fastest traverse by a specified time—for example, completing a route 30 seconds faster than their previous attempt.

Traverse for Time Sample Progress Card

Climber's name _____

Date of climb	Time on wall (minutes)	Number of horizontal laps	Number of vertical laps

From J. Stiehl and D. Chase, 2008, *Traversing walls: 68 activities on and off the wall* (Champaign, IL: Human Kinetics).

- Divide the traverse wall into five sections and assign one climber to each area. The climbers compete to stay on the wall the longest. They must keep moving and can't take long breaks to rest. At the end of the activity, the five best climbers compete in a championship round to test their endurance.

Adapted, by permission, from J. Stiehl and T.B. Ramsey, 2005, *Climbing walls: A complete guide* (Champaign, IL: Human Kinetics), 112.

Wall Obstacle Course

Overview

Climbers traverse the wall to locate obstacle course cards, then as a small group they complete the obstacle course.

Setup

Tape obstacle course cards next to various holds.

Description

This activity is designed for small groups and begins with one climber from each group traversing the wall to retrieve an obstacle course card of his choice. Once he has a card, he steps off the wall and joins his group, and they follow the instructions on the card. For example, a card might direct them to perform a set of calisthenics in another area of the gym, or it might give more specific instructions, such as "Dribble a basketball around the row of chairs, using the crossover dribble to change hands."

After the group completes the task, the next climber places the card by any unoccupied hold and then traverses to retrieve a different obstacle card. This process continues until each member of the group has retrieved an obstacle card, and the first team to complete all its tasks wins.

Variations

- Mark the obstacle cards with numbers, and roll dice to determine which card each climber must retrieve.
- Each team creates an obstacle course card and places it on the wall for other teams to retrieve.
- Time the activity. The first team to complete six obstacle courses wins.

- Expand the variety of tasks and activities on the obstacle cards. The following are examples:
  - Practice ball skills, such as dribbling, bouncing, passing, throwing at targets, shooting, rebounding, and bowling.
  - Do warm-up activities and dome cone activities.
  - Jog to a jump rope station and skip rope for 2 minutes.
  - Crab walk to a basketball station and shoot layups until each member of the team scores two baskets.
  - Traverse to the top of the wall and back, one at a time.
  - Skip to a dome cone station and help each other walk a set course.
  - Engage in mental as well as physical challenges.

Off Limits

Overview

Climbers traverse the wall without touching holds of a certain color.

Setup

Randomly place masking tape or colored tape next to at least two-thirds of the holds.

Description

This activity is designed for pairs. Each pair selects a color to be off limits and takes turns traversing the wall without touching any holds of that color. While one student traverses, the other spots. Roles change after a climber traverses to the other side of the wall.

Variations

- Climbers must traverse the route in a set time without touching the off-limits holds.
- Instead of avoiding holds of the chosen color, students can use only holds of that color.
- Climbers must traverse the route in a set time while using only holds of the chosen color.
- Instead of colors, identify the off-limits holds by other means. For example, attach playing cards to the wall, and use card numbers or suits to designate holds as off limits.

- To increase the challenge, each pair of students must declare two colors to be off limits.
- To decrease the challenge, each pair is allowed to use three of their off-limits holds.
- Students accumulate points by touching off-limits holds or stepping off the wall. At the end of the activity, the pair with the fewest points is the winner.

Peak Ascent

Overview

Climbers track their progress by transferring their distances traveled on a map or picture of a mountain.

Setup

You'll need a map or picture of a mountain trail and some pens.

Description

This activity allows climbers to track their total distances traversed on the wall. Individual climbers keep track of the number of times that they traverse from one side of the wall to the other and multiply that number by the length of the wall. For example, if a climber traverses the wall 10 times in one class period and the wall is 40 feet long, her total distance is 400 feet. At the end of the session, add all the distances together to see how far the class traversed as a whole. Draw that distance on a map of a mountain trail to represent the group's progress toward the peak.

Variations

- Keep track of horizontal and vertical distances. (You'll need to know the height of the wall as well as its length.)
- Combine this activity with other traversing activities. That is, have students keep track of their total distances while they perform other activities.
- Split the class into small teams of equal size and ability, and have the teams compete by tracking their distance on a map of a race course. For example, four teams can simulate the Tour de France.

- Assign new distances to the length and height of the wall. For example, declare that one horizontal lap counts as 1 mile or kilometer, or that one vertical lap counts as a quarter mile or kilometer. These inflated distances allow students to track their progress on longer journeys, such as a trip to the moon and back. Ask students to choose a destination. To motivate them to attempt greater distances, let them know how far other classes have gone recently.

- Students can track their progress on various kinds of maps. Here are examples:

  - On a map of their city or state, students can see how long it takes them to cross from one end to the other. See the sample map section of Colorado (figure a).

  - On a map of the country, students can see how long it takes them to travel from west to east or north to south.

  - On a picture or map of Mount Everest, students see how long it takes them to reach the summit by using vertical distances traversed on the wall.

  - On a map of Lewis and Clark's trail, students see how long it takes them to re-create that famous journey. See the sample trail map (figure b).

a

b

Road Map

Overview

Climbers locate checkpoints that teammates use to solve road map problems.

Setup

Place numbers from 1 to 9 next to some holds. You'll also need a map and a list of checkpoint sites for each group.

Description

When a climber reaches a numbered hold, she calls the number out to her teammates. They consult their map, which features a series of numbered checkpoints such as schools, lakes, and bridges (see the figure on the next page). Once they find the matching checkpoint on the map, the students determine the shortest distance to the next numbered checkpoint. Then the climber traverses to that number on the wall, and the process continues.

The group must plan a round trip that goes through all the checkpoints and brings the climber back to where she started. Along the way, they outline the route and the checkpoints on the map with crayons or markers. When the trip is complete, they measure on the map with string the distance between each checkpoint. The sum of these distances provides the total distance.

1 = High school
2 = Senior center
3 = Mall, store, or corporation
4 = Hospital (people or animal)
5 = Transit center
6 = Mobile home park
7 = Community college campus
8 = University campus
9 = City park or city hall

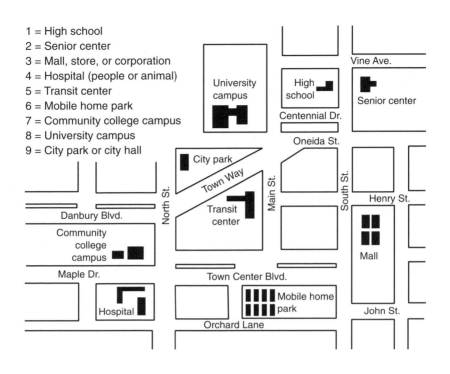

Variations

- Use actual road maps, which you can find in phone books, at fuel stations, at your local Chamber of Commerce office, at hotel front desks, and so on.
- Ask students to bring in local, state, or national maps.
- Groups compete to find the round-trip route that goes through all checkpoints.
- Increase the number of checkpoints.
- At each checkpoint, the group must glean information from the map to answer a question. They might need to provide the distance between two points, the population of a town, the name of a river crossed by a particular bridge, directions to a landmark, and so on. (You can include the answers to the questions on the back of the checkpoint lists.) Groups can also conduct follow-up research for questions, such as "Whom was this bridge named after, and why was it built?"
- Groups write questions for other teams to answer.

Spider Web

Overview

A climber traverses the wall, winding a single length of yarn around handholds while a partner on the floor feeds out slack.

Setup

You'll need yarn or string, approximately 50 feet (15 m) per climber.

Description

The climber (or "spider") traverses around the wall while gripping one end of a long piece of yarn. He loops the yarn around various handholds as he crawls, changing directions frequently so that the result looks like a spider's web. The activity ends when the climber runs out of yarn.

Variations

- To increase the challenge, the spider must avoid (or must use) holds of a certain color.
- To increase or decrease climb time, give the students longer or shorter pieces of yarn.
- The climber must create a web that resembles a square, a pentagon, a hexagon, or any other specified shape.

- The web must cross itself a specified number of times.
- The web must follow a set pattern, which is determined by holds marked with colored tape.
- Each climber has a limited time on the wall, and the new spider continues building the previous one's web.
- After a specified time (for example, when the climber has less than half of his yarn left), the partner begins traversing the wall. The partner gathers up the yarn as she goes, unmaking the web. Once she erases the entire web, partners switch roles.
- Students draw maps with routes for climbers to follow.

Adapted, by permission, from J. Stiehl and T.B. Ramsey, 2005, *Climbing walls: A complete guide* (Champaign, IL: Human Kinetics), 113.

Take-Away

Overview

Climbers take turns subtracting available holds, creating a more difficult traversing route.

Setup

Use masking tape to create a specific route on the wall.

Description

This activity is designed for multiple climbers. Each climber gets a turn practicing the route marked by the masking tape. Then the first climber traverses the route and, somewhere along the way, eliminates one hold by removing its piece of tape. Each subsequent climber follows the altered route and also removes one hold of his choice. Climbers continue until they can no longer complete the sequence. The winner is the last climber to remove a hold and complete the route.

Variations

- Climbers can use any footholds, but they can use only the specified handholds.
- The original route marks specific footholds as well as handholds, and climbers can remove either kind of hold as they traverse.
- Students on the floor use a spinner to direct climbers to remove a hold of a certain color.

- Students on the floor simply choose which holds a climber must remove.
- Number each piece of tape from 1 to 6, and let students on the floor roll a die to determine which holds are eligible to be removed by the climber. If no more holds of that number remain on the wall—for example, if the die roll is 2 but all holds marked 2 have already been removed—the climber can proceed without removing a hold or can remove another hold of her choice.
- Mark several routes with various colors of tape, and let each climber decide which route he will follow.

Pointer

Overview

Climbers follow the route pointed out by partners.

Setup

You'll need an object that can be used for pointing, such as a foam noodle.

Description

This activity is designed for partners. The climber begins traversing the wall. Before each move, the partner on the ground (the pointer) selects the climber's next hold by tapping it lightly with a foam noodle or similar object. The pointer should try to select a hold that is challenging but not too difficult. When the climber can't make the requested move, partners switch roles.

Variations

- Roles change after a specified time limit.
- A spotter or another group member can mark the holds with a piece of marking tape so that everyone gets a chance to climb the selected route.
- The pointer can call out, "Left" or "Right," before selecting the next hold. The climber must move to that hold using the hand or foot that was called.
- Instead of using a noodle or object, the pointer can call out a specific color, which allows the climber to move to any hold of that color.

- The pointer can throw a beanbag or tennis ball at the wall to indicate the next hold.

- With equally matched partners, a competitive variation allows the pointer to attempt any move that the climber can't make. If the pointer completes the move successfully, he remains on the wall, and the other student becomes the pointer. If the pointer fails, the requested move is disregarded (since neither student can do it), and the partners continue in their original roles.

- Combine this activity with Add-On or Mirroring (chapter 3). While climbers try to copy moves on the wall, another student on the floor points out each new hold.

Capital Gains

Overview

Climbers traverse the wall while identifying state capitals.

Setup

This activity is designed for a wall on which a map of the United States is painted (see the photo). If you don't have such a wall, simply create a map overlay as described on pages 26 and 27 in chapter 1.

Description

Beginning at the right side of the wall (the East Coast of the United States), a climber traverses toward the left side (the West Coast). At any point, the spotter can call out, "Capital!" and the climber has 5 seconds to identify the capital of the state currently being touched. For example, if the climber has a hand on Massachusetts when the spotter calls out, he must answer "Boston." Roles change when a climber identifies a capital incorrectly or fails to identify the capital within 5 seconds.

Variations

- Climbers must identify the capital for each state they touch.
- When prompted by the spotter, climbers must identify a unique characteristic of the state currently being touched. For example, Colorado is the home of the Rocky Mountain National Park, Wisconsin is famous for cheese, Rhode Island is the smallest state, and so on.
- When prompted by the spotter, climbers must name a professional sports team of the state currently being touched. For example, Massachusetts is home to the Boston Bruins hockey team, Illinois is home to the Chicago Bulls basketball team, California is home to the Oakland Raiders football team, and so on.
- Climbers must name one college from each state that they pass through, or the spotter can call out a college and the climber must visit that state.
- Climbers must traverse from one coast to the other visiting a series of predetermined states. For example, climbers must do the following:
  - Visit all states that begin with the letter M but not visit any states that begin with the letter C.
  - Visit the home states of certain professional sports teams.
  - Visit states that have the word *New* in their names.
  - Visit any three states of their choice and explain their reasons. For example, a climber might visit California because she likes the ocean, New York because she wants to see the Statue of Liberty, and Colorado because she enjoys skiing.
  - Visit two states that are painted purple, one state that is painted red, and three states that are painted green, naming each state as they visit.
- In pairs or small groups, students can create traverse route worksheets to be used by other climbers. Following are a few examples of traverse route worksheets.

State Trivia

Answer the following questions, and then visit the states you named in order from 1 to 10.

1. Which of the 50 states is the smallest?

2. Which of the 50 states is the largest?

3. The highest city in the USA, known as Leadville, is 10,200 feet above sea level and is found in what state?

4. Which of the 50 states is closest to Russia?

5. In which state is Mount Rushmore located?

6. Which state borders only one other state?

7. In which state is Mount Washington located?

8. In which state is the Grand Canyon located?

9. In which state were more presidents born than in any other?

10. Which of the 50 states is the only one to be named after a president?

From J. Stiehl and D. Chase, 2008, *Traversing Walls: 68 activities on and off the wall* (Champaign, IL: Human Kinetics).

State Landmarks

The following famous landmarks are associated with particular states. Name the state where each landmark is found, and then visit those states in any order.

1. Rocky Mountain National Park

2. Plymouth Rock

3. Empire State Building

4. Golden Gate Bridge

5. Pearl Harbor

6. Mount St. Helens

7. Yellowstone National Park

8. The Alamo

9. U.S. Capitol Building

10. The Everglades

From J. Stiehl and D. Chase, 2008, *Traversing Walls: 68 activities on and off the wall* (Champaign, IL: Human Kinetics).

State Nicknames

The following nicknames are associated with particular states. Name the state that goes with each nickname, and then visit those states in the shortest traverse route possible.

1. Show Me State

2. Beaver State

3. First State

4. Granite State

5. Garden State

6. Bluegrass State

7. Golden State

8. Empire State

9. Mount Rushmore State

10. Last Frontier

11. Sunflower State

12. Lone Star State

13. Aloha State

14. Heart of Dixie

15. Constitution State

16. Wolverine State

17. Peach State

18. Sunshine State

From J. Stiehl and D. Chase, 2008, *Traversing Walls: 68 activities on and off the wall* (Champaign, IL: Human Kinetics).

State Flowers

The following flowers are the official flowers of certain states. Name the state for each flower, and then visit those states using the fewest number of holds.

1. Mistletoe

2. Rocky Mountain columbine

3. Black-eyed Susan

4. Oregon grape

5. Orange blossom

6. California poppy

7. Rose

8. Sunflower

9. Bitterroot

10. Wild prairie rose

11. Scarlet carnation

12. Iris

From J. Stiehl and D. Chase, 2008, *Traversing Walls: 68 activities on and off the wall* (Champaign, IL: Human Kinetics).

Worksheet 1 Answers

1. Rhode Island
2. Alaska
3. Colorado
4. Alaska
5. South Dakota
6. Maine
7. New Hampshire
8. Arizona
9. Virginia
10. Washington

Worksheet 2 Answers

1. Colorado
2. Massachusetts
3. New York
4. California
5. Hawaii
6. Washington
7. Wyoming
8. Texas
9. Washington, D.C.
10. Florida

Worksheet 3 Answers

1. Missouri
2. Oregon
3. Delaware
4. New Hampshire
5. New Jersey
6. Kentucky
7. California
8. New York
9. South Dakota
10. Alaska
11. Kansas
12. Texas
13. Hawaii
14. Alabama
15. Connecticut
16. Michigan
17. Georgia
18. Florida

Worksheet 4 Answers

1. Oklahoma
2. Colorado
3. Maryland
4. Oregon
5. Florida
6. California
7. New York
8. Kansas
9. Montana
10. Iowa
11. Ohio
12. Tennessee

Healthy Living

The activities presented in this chapter offer a great opportunity for you to work collaboratively with other classroom teachers or recreation leaders. For instance, you can work with science teachers to develop activity questions that reflect what students are currently learning. The activities can reinforce or introduce healthy guidelines on nutrition, physical activity, and safety. In addition, some of these activities can help teach about the human body. Although students might need some prior instruction in some areas, you can modify all of the activities to make them appropriate for any given group.

Food Crossword

Overview

Climbers locate words of foods, which must be placed into a crossword puzzle and then designated by their respective food groups.

Setup

You'll need cards with names of foods placed near holds on the wall, a crossword puzzle using the same food names as answers (see page 130), and colored pencils or markers.

FOOD CROSSWORD

Fill in the words that match the picture clues.

Across

1. Green with stalks and tiny flowers
3. Sometimes popped
4. Some are red, some are green
6. Fatter at the bottom than the top
10. Found in a pod
11. One a day keeps the doctor away
12. Humpty Dumpty
13. In a loaf, but not bread
14. Look like lemons, only green

Down

1. Made with yeast
2. Bugs Bunny loves them
3. Macaroni and _____
5. New York or Chicago style?
7. Often arrives before salad
8. Bowl, fruit, milk, spoon = yum
9. Sometimes hot, sometimes sweet

Additional useful resource: www.crosswordpuzzlegames.com/create.html
A teacher can enter up to 20 words and hints (clues) to create puzzles with
various themes.

From J. Stiehl and D. Chase, 2008, *Traversing walls: 68 activities on and off the wall* (Champaign, IL: Human Kinetics).

Description

Introduce the activity with a discussion of nutrition. For example, "Just as an automobile requires fuel, we need fuel in order to run efficiently. The car uses gasoline, while we use food. Your body runs best on a variety of foods that ensure the proper balance of nutrients. So eating a variety of foods is the most healthful way to eat."

When a climber locates a card with the name of a food, she calls it out. Her teammates find the correct clue on their crossword puzzle and print the name in the appropriate spaces. After completing the puzzle, the group creates a meal by choosing one food from each of the basic food groups.

- Milk: string cheese, nonfat milk, whole milk, yogurt, ice milk, frozen yogurt
- Meat and meat alternatives: turkey, ham, hamburger, meatloaf, grilled tuna, chicken salad, soy burgers
- Grains: whole-wheat bread, hamburger bun, corn bread, bagel, pita bread, potato, corn
- Fruits and vegetables: apple, tomato, lettuce, green chilies, carrot
- Discretionary foods: chocolate cake, cola, candied yams, french fries, apple pie, cookies

Variations

- On the puzzle, circle or color those foods that are low in sugar, fat, salt, artificial colors, and other not-so-healthy ingredients.
- On the puzzle, place triangles around the foods that you eat.
- Make this activity more like Bingo by having the students record food names as the climber locates them on the wall, with a goal of creating a complete meal.
- Create word searches using online programs such as
    - http://puzzlemaker.school.discovery.com/WordSearch SetupForm.html
    - www.armoredpenguin.com/wordsearch/
    - http://freewordsearch.teacherly.com

Fill In the Muscles

Overview

Climbers locate names of muscles, which teammates then identify on a picture of a person.

Setup

You'll need names of muscles placed next to holds, a worksheet picturing the large-muscle groups of a person (see page 133), and colored pencils or markers. You may wish to consult books or Web sites for additional information.

Description

Introduce the activity with a discussion of how muscles are involved in exercise. For example:

- The construction of the body allows a wide range of possible movements requiring complex coordination.
- It is useful to understand which muscles are used to perform specific movements.
- The human body can jump, run, kick, throw, and perform a variety of movements because of its muscles and how they are attached to the skeletal system.
- Think of the skeleton as a puppet and the muscles as the strings that pull on the bones to make them move.
- The muscles receive the energy they need to work properly from the blood, which is given oxygen by the pulmonary system, pumped by the heart, and circulated through a system of vessels.

When the climber reaches a muscle name, he calls out that word. Teammates identify on their picture where that muscle is located and then insert the name of the muscle in the correct space. Once the picture is complete, they can color the worksheet.

Variations

- Add more large-muscle groups (such as deltoids, latissimus dorsi), or smaller and more slender muscles (such as brachialis, soleus).
- Insert muscle names as well as a description of its purpose on the worksheet (for example, located in the lower half of the upper arm, the brachialis protects the elbow and helps bend and rotate the forearm).

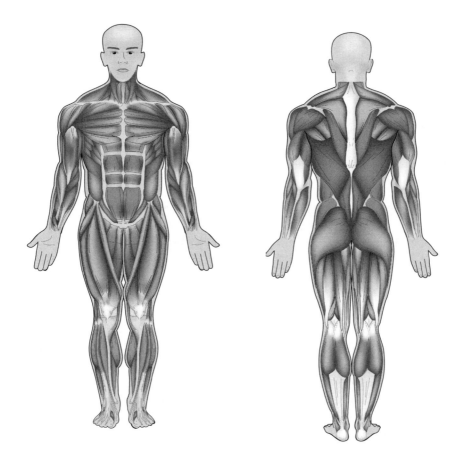

From J. Stiehl and D. Chase, 2008, *Traversing walls: 68 activities on and off the wall* (Champaign, IL: Human Kinetics). Adapted, by permission, from C. Corbin and R. Lindsey, 2005, *Fitness for life*, 5th ed. (Champaign, IL: Human Kinetics), 151-152.

- Explain and demonstrate a conditioning exercise for each muscle, and have the students perform it, too. For example, "To stretch the gastrocnemius, stand about 2 feet (60 cm) from a wall and place your hands against it. Extend one leg behind you with the knee straight. Keep your heel on the floor and lean forward until you feel a stretch in the rear leg. Hold the stretch for 20 to 30 seconds, then repeat two or three times."
- Add the skeletal system, possibly including tendons and ligaments.
- Add the cardiovascular and pulmonary system.

MyPyramid

Overview

Climbers retrieve wall cards labeled with various foods, and groups place the foods in their proper places on a MyPyramid diagram.

Setup

Next to handholds, tape pictures of various foods from all food groups (corn, apple, elbow macaroni). You'll also need masking tape and a MyPyramid diagram (see page 135).

Description

Designed for small teams, this activity requires knowledge of the USDA food guide pyramid, MyPyramid. Students can learn about MyPyramid at the official Web site (www.mypyramid.gov) or draw from their classroom knowledge.

In each team, the students decide which member's MyPyramid diagram to complete. Taking turns, climbers traverse the wall for cards labeled with the name of foods needed for the diagram. Upon finding a card, the climber brings it to her team, and the students write the name of that food in the correct spot on the diagram. Then the next climber returns the card to any nonlabeled hold and traverses the wall to find another card.

Variety is the key to a healthy diet, so no team can retrieve the same labeled food card more than once. Using the fruits group as an example, if an apple is selected as one serving, apple may not be selected again as another serving (but orange or banana would be fine). The game ends when all teams have retrieved the proper number of servings from each of the recommended food groups.

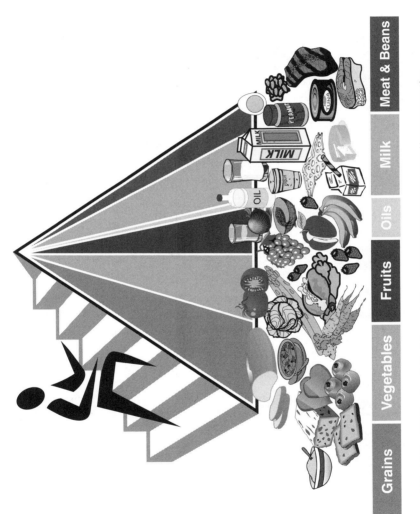

From J. Stiehl and D. Chase, 2008, *Traversing walls: 68 activities on and off the wall* (Champaign, IL: Human Kinetics). Reprinted from www.mypyramid.gov.

Variations

- Using tape, outline one giant pyramid shape on the wall to represent MyPyramid around the holds. Then climbers randomly pick labeled food cards from a box and place them on the wall in the appropriate spot.

- Place cards or the pyramid shape higher up on the wall to increase climbing time.

- Have the students create the labeled food cards as an off-wall activity.

- To test the students' knowledge about MyPyramid, cover the categories at the bottom of the diagram on page 135 before photocopying it. Can they still place the foods in the proper sections of the pyramid?

- Include calories on the labeled food cards and have teams create a balanced diet for a specified caloric intake.

- Create (or have students create) a collection of pictures of foods from each group. When climbers locate cards on the wall, they call out the food names, and their teammates complete the MyPyramid diagram by finding matching pictures of those foods instead of just writing down the names.

Body Systems

Overview

Climbers locate tissues and organs for various body systems (for example, digestive, cardiovascular, respiratory), which teammates identify on a body outline.

Setup

Next to holds, place names of tissues and organs for body systems. You'll also need a worksheet picturing an outline of a body (see page 137), and colored pencils or markers. You may wish to consult books or Web sites for additional body examples.

Description

This activity is designed for small groups and requires knowledge of human body systems. One climber from each group traverses the wall for cards labeled with the names of tissues and organs. Upon finding a card, the climber brings it to his team, and the students write the name of the tissue or organ in the correct spot on their body outline sheet. Then a different climber returns the card to any nonlabeled hold and traverses the wall to find another card. This process continues until each team has marked all the tissues or organs on their body outline sheet.

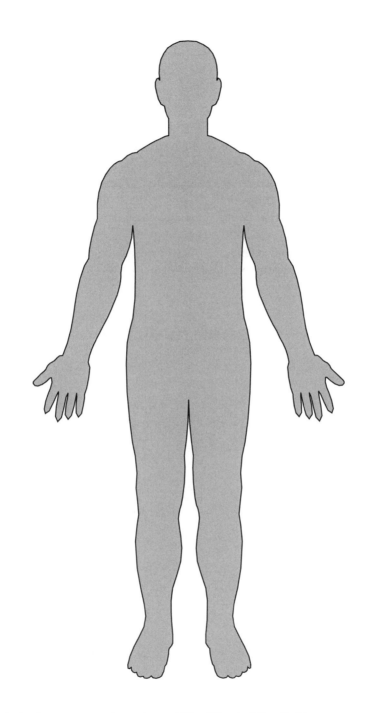

From J. Stiehl and D. Chase, 2008, *Traversing walls: 68 activities on and off the wall* (Champaign, IL: Human Kinetics).

Variations

- Students can draw the tissues and organs on their body outline sheet instead of simply recording the names.
- Add descriptions of tissue and organ functions to the cards. For example, the stomach card might say that it absorbs water, churns food, and secretes digestive enzymes.
- Create cards that feature pictures of tissues and organs instead of their names.
- Tape a rough outline of a body around the holds or create a map overlay (see pages 26-27 in chapter 1 for details). Climbers randomly choose pictures of tissues or organs from a box and place them on the wall in the appropriate spot.
- Increase the complexity of a system by breaking it down into smaller parts. For example, include the heart structure as part of the cardiovascular system.

Bones Galore

Overview

Climbers locate names of skeletal bones, which teammates then identify on a picture of a skeleton.

Setup

Next to holds, place names of skeletal bones. You'll also need a worksheet picturing a skeleton (see page 139), and colored pencils or markers. You may wish to consult books or Web sites for additional skeleton examples.

Description

This activity is designed for small groups and requires knowledge of the human skeletal system. One climber from each group traverses the wall for cards labeled with the names of major bones. Upon finding a card, the climber brings it to her team, and the students write the name of the bone in the correct spot on their skeleton sheet. Then a different climber returns the card to any nonlabeled hold and traverses the wall to find another card. This process continues until each team has marked all the major bones on their respective skeleton sheet.

Adjust the number of bones in the activity according to the students' level of knowledge. For example, older students (grades 7-12) should be able to

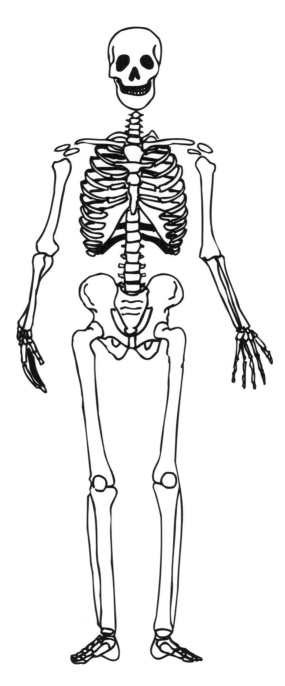

From J. Stiehl and D. Chase, 2008, *Traversing walls: 68 activities on and off the wall* (Champaign, IL: Human Kinetics).

fill in 50 bones, while elementary students (grades K-6) should be able to fill in 10 bones.

Variations

- Provide hula hoops to each team. When a climber locates each bone card, her teammates twirl the hoops on their own matching body part. For example, if the climber finds the tibia or fibula bone, her teammates twirl the hoop on their lower legs. After twirling the hoops correctly, the teammates write the bone on their skeleton sheet.

- Teams collect the bones of horses or other animals they've studied in science class.

- Provide a three-dimensional skeleton (similar to those found in many middle school science classes) and challenge the entire class to record all the skeletal bones as quickly as possible, with as few mistakes as possible. Require that each student traverse the wall at least once to retrieve a bone card.

- Combine this activity with Fill In the Muscles (see page 132) to promote a greater understanding of the relationship between bones and muscles. Specifically, students can see how bones and muscles work together during traversing activities to help them maintain their balance, maximize their power, and reduce fatigue when resting on a climbing hold.

Pathways to Health

Overview

Climbers traverse the wall within a predetermined route (marked with string), stopping at health behavior cards for further instructions.

Setup

You'll need dice, masking tape, string, double-sided Velcro tape, and health behavior cards. Using two pieces of string or yarn, create a meandering route from one side of the wall to the other (see page 142 for three sample routes). Health behavior cards are taped next to handholds within the marked path; starting and ending points are indicated with masking tape. An excellent activity for older students is designing health behavior cards for younger students.

Description

Each player starts a turn by rolling a die to determine the number of climbing moves to make within the marked climbing area (for example, if climber 1 rolls a 6, he would have to make 6 climbing moves within the area marked by string). A climbing move is defined as moving any body part from one hold to another. After the climber has made the appropriate number of moves indicated by the roll of a die, the climber reads a health behavior card that is taped to one of the holds he is touching and follows the instructions. For example, a card might say, "Name two benefits of exercise and celebrate those benefits off the wall by performing 10 jumping jacks or 15 sit-ups with a friend."

The next time the climber traverses the wall, he begins at the location of the last health behavior card he read. Climbers can place pieces of masking tape with their names on the wall to help them remember where they left off.

Variations

- Change what constitutes a move. For example, the number determined by the die roll refers only to hand moves (or foot moves). This increases the distance traversed in each turn.

- Instead of beginning at the last card location, start at the original starting point on subsequent turns. Climb past the last card location to the next one.

- Vary the difficulty of the route. The first sample route (figure *a*) is a basic route requiring both hands and feet to remain in the designated area. The second sample route (figure *b*) requires that only hands remain in the designated area. The third sample route (figure *c*) requires that only the feet remain in the designated area. Route difficulty depends on the number and location of holds inside and outside the designated areas. For instance, a narrow area designated for hands only could be challenging if it contains easy handholds but few or difficult footholds. Conversely, it might be just as challenging if it contains small, difficult handholds but has many reasonable footholds.

- Use the placement of the cards to determine the level of difficulty.

- Introduce consequences for incorrect answers. For example, climbers might lose a turn, go back to the last card they answered correctly, or start the whole route over again.

- Group health behavior cards into categories, such as physical activity, nutrition, stress management, oral health, and personal hygiene. Sample questions for each of these categories appear on page 143.

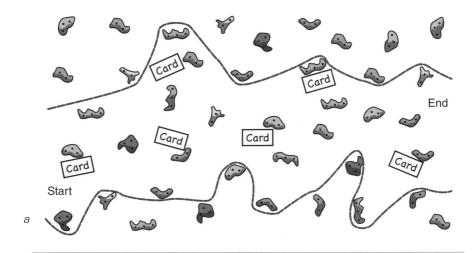

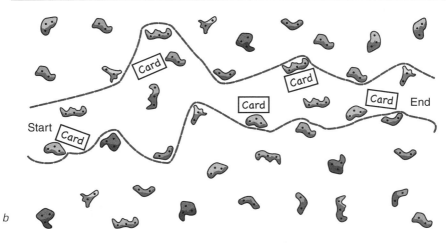

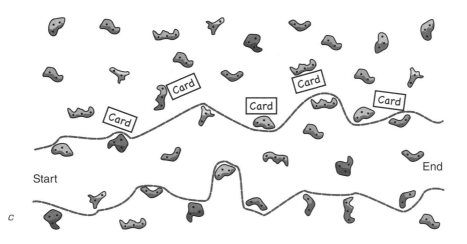

Physical Activity Questions

- Name two things that could happen if you don't engage in regular physical activity. (Answer: You could gain weight and be at an increased risk for heart disease.)
- Why does your heart rate increase when you exercise? (Answer: It needs to pump more blood and oxygen to your body.)

Nutrition Questions

- According to MyPyramid, if you take in 2,000 calories per day, how many cups of vegetables are recommended daily? (Answer: 2.5 cups.)
- True or false: Foods such as butter and cream cheese, which are made from milk but have little to no calcium content, are not part of the milk group. (Answer: True.)

Stress Management Questions

- Name two things you can do to relax when you feel stressed. (Answer: Do slow, deep breathing exercises, or sit in a quiet room and listen to soft music.)
- What are two negative effects of failing to manage stress? (Answer: Anxiety and lack of sleep.)

Oral Health Questions

- What two things should you do daily to keep your teeth in good health? (Answer: Brush and floss.)
- True or false: If you visit the dentist regularly, you don't need to brush your teeth. (Answer: False.)

Personal Hygiene Questions

- If you're helping your parents cook dinner and you cut raw chicken, should you wash your hands before or after handling the meat? (Answer: Both.)
- If two people share hats or combs, what might spread from one person to the next? (Answer: Head lice.)

- Use scenario cards that involve making choices about health behaviors. Each card presents a situation and describes the consequences of making good choices and bad choices. See the following sample scenario cards.

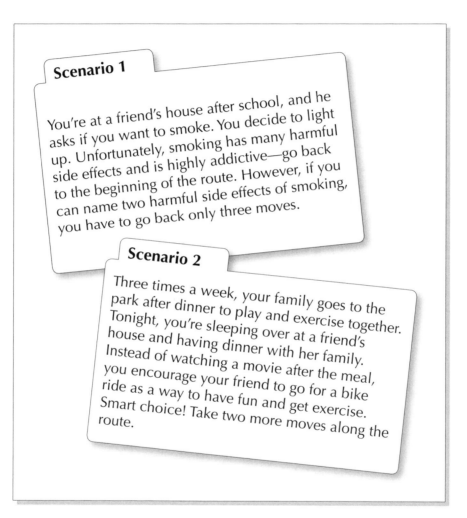

Scenario 1

You're at a friend's house after school, and he asks if you want to smoke. You decide to light up. Unfortunately, smoking has many harmful side effects and is highly addictive—go back to the beginning of the route. However, if you can name two harmful side effects of smoking, you have to go back only three moves.

Scenario 2

Three times a week, your family goes to the park after dinner to play and exercise together. Tonight, you're sleeping over at a friend's house and having dinner with her family. Instead of watching a movie after the meal, you encourage your friend to go for a bike ride as a way to have fun and get exercise. Smart choice! Take two more moves along the route.

- If climbers answer a question correctly or make a positive behavior choice, require them to perform some kind of physical activity before moving on. For example, a card can instruct climbers to traverse to the top of the wall and back before making the next move along the route.

A Word From Our Sponsor

Overview

Climbers locate numbers that correspond to items that teammates use to create and then market a new fictitious product.

Setup

Place numbers from 1 to 9 next to some holds. You'll also need a list of product items (for example, 1 = milk carton, 2 = marking pen, 3 = balloon, 4 = tennis racket) for each group, and a container of those items.

Description

While traversing the wall, a climber reaches several numbered holds. She calls each number to her teammates, who select items with the matching number from the large collection of objects. After gathering all specified items, the team must use some or all of the objects to develop a fictitious product. For example, if they choose colored paper, a rubber glove, a marking pen, and a small cardboard box, they might use the items to create a milk carton. They can wrap the paper around the box, draw a funny label on the paper, and attach the glove to the bottom of the carton to represent a cow's udder.

Encourage students to use their creativity and develop a flashy, appealing product. They can invent a snappy slogan, a humorous list of contents, special instructions for using the product, or a testimonial from a satisfied customer.

Variations

- Creating the packaging is only part of the process. Each group can write or present a commercial to show off their new product. Encourage slogans, jingles, and skits.

- Ask members of other teams to offer positive comments about the products and commercials.

- Give each team an empty container (such as a cereal box, a large can, or a paper bag) and have them redecorate it to show off their new product. Be sure to provide paper, glue, scissors, paints, colored string, or any needed materials.

- Instead of creating a product, each team develops a game that uses the items, complete with a name and a set of rules. Teams write out the details to hand in, demonstrate their games to the class, or switch games with other teams.

APPENDIX: RESOURCES

Suppliers

Many of the following sites can direct you to vendors for traverse-wall design, construction, and equipment. For updated listings, see http://dmoz.org/Business/Consumer_Goods_and_Services/Recreation/Outdoors/Climbing/Holds_and_Walls.

- First Ascent Climbing Walls: www.firstascentclimbingwalls.com
- Palos Sports: www.palossports.com
- Gopher: www.gophersport.com
- Flaghouse: www.flaghouse.com
- Toledo Physical Education Supply: www.tpesonline.com
- Great Lakes Sports: www.greatlakessports.com
- Sportime: www.sportime.com
- Sportwall International: www.sportwall.com
- US-Games: www.us-games.com
- Wolverine Sports: www.wolverinesports.com
- Adventure Hardware: www.adventurehardware.com
- High 5: www.high5adventure.org
- Project Adventure: www.pa.org

Associations and Professional Support and Information Sites

- Association for Challenge Course Technology (ACCT): www.acctinfo.org
- Climbing Wall Association: www.climbingwallindustry.org

BIBLIOGRAPHY

Hurni, M. (2003). *Coaching climbing.* Guilford, CT: Falcon.

Hyder, M. (1999). Have your students been climbing the walls: The growth of indoor climbing. *Journal of Physical Education, Recreation, and Dance, 70*(9), 32-36.

Leubben, C. (2002). *Betty and the silver spider: Welcome to gym climbing.* Boulder, CO: Sharp End.

Long, J. (1994). *Gym climb.* Evergreen, CO: Chockstone Press.

Mellor, D. (1997). *Rock climbing: A trailside guide.* New York: Norton.

National Association for Sport and Physical Education. (2004). *Moving into the future: National standards for physical education* (2nd ed.). Reston, VA: Author.

Steffen, J., & Stiehl, J. (1995). Does your gym have six walls? *Journal of Physical Education, Recreation, and Dance, 66*(8), 43-47.

Stiehl, J., & Ramsey, T. (2005). *Climbing walls: A complete guide.* Champaign, IL: Human Kinetics.

ABOUT THE AUTHORS

Jim Stiehl, PhD, is a professor at the School of Sport and Exercise Science at the University of Northern Colorado (UNC). Stiehl is a climbing instructor and challenge course director at UNC and has worked with kids and teachers for the past 20 years on traverse walls, indoor climbing walls, ropes courses, and rock climbing.

Stiehl is former chair of the Council on Outdoor Education for the American Alliance for Health, Physical Education, Recreation and Dance (AAHPERD). He was named Scholar of the Year in 1993 for the Central District Association of HPERD and has received several research and writing excellence awards. He resides in Greeley, Colorado, with his wife, Julie, and enjoys backpacking and hiking, backcountry skiing and snowshoeing, and rock climbing and mountaineering in his leisure time.

Dan Chase, MS, is a teaching assistant and is completing his PhD at the School of Sport and Exercise Science at the University of Northern Colorado. Along with Dr. Stiehl, he has been working with kids for the past 10 years on traverse walls, climbing walls, rock climbing, and ropes courses. Mr. Chase is a member of NIRSA and AAHPERD and has been a lead facilitator on the UNC Challenge Course. He lives in Loveland, Colorado, with his wife, Lisa, and likes to rock climb, road cycle, hike, and backpack in his spare time.